Stories on the Journey:
A Homiletic Biography
(Cycle A Homilies)

Stories on the Journey: A Homiletic Biography
(Cycle A Homilies)

Rev. Peter G. Jankowski

Stories on the Journey:
A Homiletic Biography
(Cycle A Homilies)

© Rev. Peter G. Jankowski 2016

All rights reserved. Without limiting the rights under copyright reserved above, no part of this publication may be reproduced, stored in a retrieval system, or transmitted, in any form or by any means (electronic, mechanical, photocopying, recording or otherwise), without the prior written permission of the copyright owner of this book.

Published by
Lighthouse Christian Publishing
SAN 257-4330
5531 Dufferin Drive
Savage, Minnesota, 55378
United States of America

www.lighthousechristianpublishing.com

Dedicated to Zaida Zelinda Jankowski & Rev. Thomas Kane - the two people who encouraged my call to the priesthood in my early years of formation.

Much thanks as well to Very Rev. Joseph Tapella from the Tribunal Office (Diocese of Joliet, IL) who edited this book for content.

Foreword
Homilies for Advent 1
Homilies for Christmas 19
Homilies for Lent & Holy Week 40
Homilies for Easter.. 79
Homilies for Ordinary Time 112
Endnotes 263
Bibliography 269

Foreword

Way back in my seminary days, I was a student at the Catholic University in Washington, D.C., studying philosophy in preparation for what was yet to come. During one of my Christmas breaks from school in 1987, I was driving my old and tarnished 1971 Volkswagen Superbeetle from Washington, D.C. to my hometown of Sandwich, Illinois (which is located about an hour and a half southwest of Chicago).

I loved my "bug" – I became an expert at fixing all the holes in the car's rusted-out floor, I rigged up an electric fan to provide my own form of air conditioning in my rust bucket during the summer months and I even learned how to tune up the VW and all that mechanical stuff. When you love something as much as I did this old bug, then you learn how to take care of it as well as you can.

I particularly remember working on my car at the St. Vincent/St. Joseph home in Freeport, Illinois, listening to classic rock music from that particular era on the radio while tuning up my engine and learning how to grind down the cylinder heads of my car. I spent hours listening to the type of music that was popular during that time – Huey Lewis, the Bangles and a lot of other forgettable music that no longer is forgettable to me.

That particular December in 1987, I was preparing for the fourteen-hour drive from Washington, D.C. back home, knowing that the road conditions would be horrific. Not only did I start my drive at night (which is the best time to drive because very few people travelled through the night... and most were smart enough not to drive in a snowstorm, anyway), the white stuff was coming down in droves.

Prior to the trip, I had just pulled out the engine of my car to grind down the cylinder heads AGAIN (I didn't say I was a great mechanic, just a mechanic) and when I put the engine back into the car, I felt that this machine was as fine-tuned as an old car could ever be. I had my musical cassette tapes in the car and in the darkest time of the night, I was on my happy way through Virginia, Maryland and the Pennsylvania mountains.

Three states into the trip, however, I noticed a light blinking on my dashboard that shined brightly on that cold winter's night. I came to find out that my battery was losing its charge as I continue to drive. When I saw the light, I thought to myself that nothing could be wrong with the car; I myself had tuned the car to perfection and I was a self-proclaimed "master mechanic." But the light paid no attention to me like a buzzing fly that did everything possible to spoil an otherwise enjoyable drive.

At first, I did not pay attention to the light. Then the glow seemed to take offense at me and shone that much brighter. Further and further up the mountains, the dashboard became an irritant to me. Two states and eight hours later, I began to panic.

With God's help (and a bunch of worn out rosary beads), I reached the border between Ohio and Indiana at two o'clock in the morning. By this time, the visibility on the road was practically nil and my car was gasping its last breath. Luckily for me, I noticed a sign for an Indiana Oasis (or whatever they are called in Indiana) and cajoled my car into moving forward just a few more feet. Like the little engine that could, so did my car, collapsing at the gas pump without any battery juice left within itself to move.

The only person at the Oasis was another traveler, about 35 years old, who was filling up his shiny brand new, navy blue Oldsmobile with Super Unleaded as he watched my predicament from a distance. After surveying the predicament for a while, "Oldsmobile Man" realized that I was in a hopeless situation and offered to recharge my battery from the battery of his own car, which I gladly accepted. After a few minutes, Oldsmobile Man asked me if I wanted him to follow me for a while down the road. Although I was glad for his help, I also realized I was talking to a stranger at two o'clock in the morning, right in the middle of a snowstorm. All I wanted to do at that moment was to pour back into my rust bucket of a Volkswagen and pray that I would get back home in one piece.

As it would have it, five miles past the Oasis, my car died for good. I came to found out a few days later that this soon-to-be priest was no brilliant mechanic; I did not have enough sense to secure the battery charge cable to its proper slot. As I was driving, the cable popped loose and caught itself in the fan belt, only to be shredded into bits. So at two o'clock in the morning, in the dark of the night, in the midst of a horrendous snowstorm, there I was stuck in the middle of nowhere – I had no cell phone (they didn't exist at the time), no one was in sight and I felt there would be no hope for me from the snowy mess in which I put myself.

I sat in the car for a while, thinking about what I had done wrong. I had a few words with God, a few with myself and I traced back every single thing I had done to get this car up and running. I was a 22-year-old novice car engineer who had all the answers, but was stuck in a blizzard with nothing but questions.

It was then, in the midst of my hopelessness, that the Oldsmobile Man who charged my battery at the Oasis had pulled up behind me. Fortunately for me, this Good Samaritan had less faith in my mechanic skills than I did and followed me on a hunch. Noticing my predicament, the Oldsmobile Man pulled up behind me, took my battery out of the car, brought me to the next rest stop where he paid a gas station to recharge the battery fully and then treated me to dinner.

While I was calming myself down from what turned out to be one of the most frantic days of my life, I encountered a kind-hearted person with a level head. The man introduced himself as Mark and told me that he lived in Silver Spring, Maryland with his wife and two kids. As an associate in an East Coast consulting firm, Mark was on his way to Chicago for some business and, like me, very much enjoyed the quiet drive of the night.

As the dinner concluded, Mark brought me to the gas station and picked up my fully charged battery. He then drove me back ten miles to put the battery into my car. When I was about to pull away, thinking the story was over, Mark went beyond his way to cap off this unbelievable story.

For five more hours on this trip, the Oldsmobile Man decided to follow behind me all the way to my home, past his Chicago destination and straight to my house in Sandwich, Illinois. Because car phones were not common in 1987, Mark would communicate with me by flashing his high beams and I would return the favor by waving my hands. Whenever my battery began to lose its charge during the trip, I'd pull off to the side of the road and he swapped the charged battery from his blue Olds with my own. For five hours, I was witnessing the Good Samaritan Story and a wonderful lesson in my faith journey.

When I finally reached my destination, I was dumbfounded. I could not understand why this very well-to-do man with the blue Olds would help me. As we reached the end of the trip, I offered this gentleman a gratuity in thanksgiving, but Mark refused to accept the gift. In response to my gesture, he said (and this I will *never* forget), "I helped you out because this is a great story. Now I can share this experience with my family and friends when I get back to Maryland."

After a little prodding, he accepted some coffee and pastries from the house before he went on his way, never to be seen again. Now every time I hear a Huey Lewis tape, I think about the man from Maryland who took a chance with this lousy mechanic and came out with a great story of faith to tell his kids. I too, had a story to share with others, a story that connects to one of our gospel passages that reads,

> For I was hungry and you gave me food, I was thirsty and you gave me drink, a stranger and you welcomed me, naked and you clothed me, ill and you cared for me, in prison and you visited me.' Then the righteous will answer Him and say, 'Lord, when did we see you hungry and feed you, or thirsty and give you drink? When did we see you a stranger and welcome you, or naked and clothe you? When did we see you ill or in prison and visit

you?' The king will say to them in reply, 'Amen, I say to you, whatever you did for one of these least brothers of mine, you did for me' (Mt 25: 35-40).

What I learned from this story, what I learn from my life, is that the canonical degree I possess does not make me a great theologian but I have learned to embrace the gift of story. Of all the ways that Christ chose to communicate with us, he chose the form of story as well. The constant theme of humility presented by our Lord and modeled on the cross provides me with the type of model I need to follow, both to be a good communicator and for my own salvation.

If nothing else, my prayer is that the personal stories presented in this book flesh out the message of our scripture readings in a contemporary, practical way that connects my life experiences with the teachings of the faith. We are taught that in every generation, life and love mandates us to return to the scripture and the interpretations of scripture (the tradition, so to speak) in order to understand what God is saying to us today. As I very much have learned, GM no longer makes Oldsmobiles but the image of the Oldsmobile man is securely cemented now in my prayer life.

May these stories be of benefit to you as they are to me. Thank you for allowing me to share my faith story with you.

Rev. Peter G. Jankowski

Stories on the Journey: The Season of Advent (Cycle A Homilies)

1st Sunday of Advent (Is 2: 1-5; Ps 122: 1-2, 3-4a, 4b-5, 6-7, 8-9; Rm 13: 11-14; Ps 85: 8; Mt 24: 37-44)

The subject matter for this weekend's readings was quite difficult for me. I have been a priest for now almost twenty years. As a priest, I have passed through the first Sunday of Advent a good number of times. Although our gospel on the first Sunday of Advent rotates between three gospels each time we pass through it (from Matthew to Mark to Luke and then back to Matthew this year), on this particular Sunday we hear yet the same message from a gospel evangelist on which I seem to drone week after week: *Be alert for the presence of the Lord and prepare yourself well because the Lord's second coming will be like that of a thief coming to your house in the middle of the night.*

In my quest to provide a fresh take on this subject, I turned to *The Jerome Biblical Commentary* for a unique take on the subject that I might not yet have addressed with you. Concerning today's gospel story, the commentary writes,

> The disciples are warned against that interest in secular business that makes them forget the *Parousia* (or Judgment Day when the Lord returns to earth a second time). The saying may originally have referred more precisely to the fall of Jerusalem rather than to the *Parousia*. The *Parousia* will manifest the difference between men—a difference that is not now apparent. Two men plowing or two women grinding meal share the same occupation and look alike externally, but God knows the difference and will make it clear.

The precise meaning of "taken" and "left" is not made clear, nor need it be. Those who are "taken" will be taken because they are ready; they have shown the vigilance that is recommended.[i]

In reflection, I began to reflect on the manner in which I have prepared myself for this presence of the Lord. At times, I sometimes wonder if my dog has more faith and gratitude in his appreciation for me than I have at times for my relationship with God, which should be infinitely more important to me. Do I seek out God in the middle of the night? Do I show the face of God in the course of the things that I do? The middle of the night serves as a deep time of introspection for a very intense priest who wishes to do as well as he can with the gospel message with the gifts he has been given by God.

Through all of this soul searching, God provided me with an answer that took place the Monday before Thanksgiving. I recalled that on THAT particular day, our parish was distributing over 75 Thanksgiving dinners to the needy of our area. As we distributed these dinners to the needy families of our community, I was bustling about, doing all the things a pastor does, I guess. As I was spinning around, I noticed that the line of families who wished to receive these dinners extended from the side door of our office all the way to the back of our garage. I spent a couple minutes with the families in need when one woman, older in age but extremely young in spirit, made this hyperactive priest stop in his tracks because she wanted to take a moment to stare at me. I asked the woman why she was burning me with her penetrating gaze and she responded,

"Because I wanted to see the face of God," to which I responded, "Thank you, I guess, but you might want to keep on looking..."

The woman's comment stopped me in my tracks, though and made me pause. I do not consider myself a saint – far from it – and I do not consider my life to be the perfect reflection of God – I pray that God is nowhere near as intense as I am. After that moment, though, I could not help but conclude that for that woman, she saw the face of God in a person who was undeserving to be attached to that connection but was connected to the presence of God nevertheless.

We really never know how Christian charity affects people at times. I sometimes don't realize how the faithful members of our parish live out their faith on a daily basis because I am so caught up in the busy, profane work of life that I overlook the faith that makes its way through those in the parish. I sometimes do not realize how those in need love us for the kind acts that we do because, for them, what we take for granted means everything in the world to them.

When the woman from a Food Pantry line reminded me about this important gift of faith, I came to a better understanding from today's gospel reading that very much associates to what I do: to be alert is likened to showing the face of God to others on a constant basis. When our lives are lived as if we are a mirror that reflects the life of God, then we are ready to spend the rest of our lives with the Lord. There may be no physical difference between two women grinding meal or the two men plowing, but God can see in our hearts. If our hearts reflect the love of God in all that we do, then we are ready for God's second coming, which is the same theme on which St. Pope Leo the Great preached some 1600 years ago when he wrote,

> Let (the soul) remember that it owes its first love to God and the second to its neighbor and all its affections must be governed by this rule, so that it departs neither from the service of the Lord, nor from what profits our fellow servant.[ii]

If we can serve as "the face of God" for the needy within our local area, then we have done our job – we have lived our ministry and we have shown the face of God to those in need. This is neither trivial nor should it be placed as secondary to any commercial or other human needs. To serve the neediest in our society is to serve God and to serve God and our neighbor is to be like God. Let us learn the lessons well from our intimate reflections of the faith in the middle of the night. May we learn to show the face of God, deeply and lovingly, to the people that we meet. This is our prayer.

2nd Sunday of Advent (Is 11: 1-10; Ps 72: 1-2, 7-8, 12-13, 17; Rm 15: 4-9; Mt 3: 1-12)

The inspiration for today's homily comes from a dead plant sitting in my deacon's office. Being of the lazy staff member variety when it comes to December decorations, Deacon Paul decided to make a statement this year in the Rectory Office by taking a branch of an artificial tree, shoving it into a dead log and putting a couple of ornaments on it, claiming that the tree reflects his contribution to the holiday spirit at St. Patrick's Church.

Upon seeing this weak attempt at a Christmas tree, most of the staff decided to give ol' Ebenezer Paul a hard time about his gift to the staff. Last week, I heard the words "lazy," "cheap," and "Charlie Brown Tree" most utilized in discussing what Deacon Paul had done (of course, most of those things were said by me, because I love to give Deacon Paul a hard time). In reality, Deacon Paul is my hero – I am just as lazy when it comes to Christmas decorations as he is. I love the season but I do not enjoy putting up the decorations and I certainly do not enjoy taking them down. My idea of decorating at Christmastime is cutting open the garbage bag that was wrapped over last year's Christmas tree, plugging the tree in and moving on with life. For this reason, I bribed my staff and the second graders of St. Patrick's School with hot chocolate in return for strung lights and hung candy canes. As a result, my small office Christmas tree has now become a mini-shrine to the Chicago Cubs (our second grade school children are all going to heaven...).

I was thinking about this "Charlie Brown Tree" for today's homily because I wanted to contrast it to a little Norfolk Pine that St. Nicholas has offered the staff at every parish I have served since my first year of ordination. Each year it takes St. Nick awhile to find enough of these mini-Christmas trees for the entire staff – in fact, he usually has to drive about 45 minutes in the middle of the night to an unspecified location to snatch up enough of these trees before the onslaught of shoppers make off with them. For everything the staff does for the priest's respective parishes, they deserve a whole lot more than these Norfolk Pines could ever symbolize.

As I said, each year St. Nick likes to visit the teachers on his feast day of December 6th to gift them with these small evergreens. I notice that a couple weeks after Christmas, these trees often come to an unfortunate end. Our resident parish horticulturalist informed me this year that Norfolk Pines usually do not survive an Illinois winter.

It is an interesting image to me, this image of the small, fragile tree, because in my reflection it is this Norfolk Pine that best represents the life of the faithful Catholic during the Advent Season. I suspect that most of us would rather follow the path of the Charlie Brown Tree than that of the Norfolk Pine because the Charlie Brown Tree is easy to maintain – it is dead. All you have to do is shove the dead branch into a dead stump, show it to the public for a few weeks and then bury it in the attic for eleven more months before you have to bring it out again. With the Charlie Brown Tree there is no watering, no manual for caring and it serves its purpose in order for us to celebrate the minimalist form of Christmas faith possible.

The Norfolk Pine, on the other hand, takes a whole lot more work and constantly depends on the care of its owner to keep the thing alive. Even with the proper watering and care and nutrients and sunlight, this Norfolk Pine may not make it to the summer because the work needed to sustain it is too overbearing for most. After a while, most people give up on the living tree and ultimately prefer to have the dead one.

Today's first reading from Isaiah serves as a reminder to us that when a plant is nourished properly and with great love, in this case the love and protection of God, the shoot of Jesse grows into a tree that branches out and gives life to the likes of King David, King Solomon and ultimately the King of Kings, the Christ-child in the manger. From this shoot of Jesse comes the life of the world that continually wishes to sustain and protect us in our own lives. It is this same theme that John the Baptist echoes in today's gospel, an image of a plant taking root when one allows the divine to nourish it.

As I reflected upon this theme, I decided to look into the scriptural references from the Bible that refer to the idea of God's planting His chosen people in order to care for them. The Second Book of Samuel (2 Sm 7: 10 specifically) and the First Book of Chronicles (1 Chr 17: 9) offer a positive approach concerning the planting of God's chosen people upon this earth. As the respective texts say to us,

> I will assign a place for my people Israel and I will plant them in it to dwell there; they will never again be disturbed, nor shall the wicked ever again oppress them, as they did at the beginning and from the day when I appointed judges over my people Israel. I will give you rest from all your enemies. Moreover, the LORD also declares to you that the LORD will make a house for you: when your days have been completed and you rest with your ancestors, I will raise up your offspring after you, sprung from your loins and I will establish His kingdom.[iii]

Rev. Peter G. Jankowski

The book of Jeremiah, written after the exile of God's chosen people from the Promised Land, reminds the faithful that the land in which they had once been planted easily can be taken away from them by the divine, due to their lack of faith. In the following text, Jeremiah reminds the faithful that if they seek purification from the Lord, then they will be cleansed and replanted back into the Promised Land, where they shall find peace:

> Thus says the LORD, the God of Israel: Like these good figs, I will also regard with favor Judah's exiles whom I sent away from this place into the land of the Chaldeans. I will look after them for good and bring them back to this land, to build them up, not tear them down; to plant them, not uproot them. I will give them a heart to know me, that I am the LORD. They shall be my people and I will be their God, for they shall return to me with their whole heart.[iv]

As we journey through this Second Sunday of Advent towards the light of our Lord's coming, we remind ourselves that the Advent Season is one of darkness, of a darkness searching for this oncoming light. If we are true to the Advent Season, we realize that without this light, we become as dead as the Charlie Brown tree sitting in our midst. Without this light, the Christmas Season becomes some type of secular, commercial-like moment that will pass away on December 26 with no eternal salvation attached to it at all.

As a people of faith, we realize that when we embrace this life and allow our lives to be nourished and maintained, this small tree, a parallel of the mustard seed parable from the thirteenth chapter of Matthew's gospel, takes root and becomes something greater than we could ever imagine.

So in the life of faith, I offer you this visual as a reflection within our Advent Season: Which of these potted trees do we wish our faith lives to represent? Which of these two evergreens represent our faith lives at the present moment? Regardless of the answer, today our Lord gives all of us an opportunity to turn to the life of grace, to the world of the divine. For those who are alive, the Lord continues to shower His life to nourish the plant; for those whose faith lives appear dead, the Lord offers the opportunity to bring the dead back into life.

May we nourish our faith lives now before it is too late. May we truly prepare ourselves for the Vine Grower – the Bread of Life – the Christ-child – who wishes to care for us and nourish us all the days of our life. This is the way we allow our faith lives to grow. This is our prayer.

3rd Sunday of Advent (Is 35: 1-6a, 10; Ps 146: 6c-7, 8-9a, 9b-10; Ja 5: 7-10; Mt 11: 2-11)

My inspiration for today's Mass came from my 45-minute wait at the Gyropractor on Friday. I call the back doctor my "Gyropractor" due to the horrible pun I assigned to him, his office being located right next to a Greek Fast Food Restaurant which I often frequent. I used to think it would be cool if my doctor bought the fast food place adjacent to his business so that I could get my back fixed and then head next door for lunch on the same visit. Obviously, my pathetic gift for bad puns is getting the best of me...

Anyhow, I had to wait forty-five minutes on Friday for an appointment that never took place. The appointment was set for 10:30 but I had an appointment back at the parish at 11:30, so by 11:15 I no longer could wait for the doctor to work on my back. This really didn't bother me, though – the doctor is a really good person and I usually spend the extra time falling asleep on the vibrating massage chair in his waiting room. Sometimes I wonder if the sleep I get in his office each week is more important than the chiropractic work, although I usually feel much better after Dr. Cissell tends to my back.

I ended up having a similar experience at my heart doctor a week or two ago. My family doctor asked me to take a stress test to make sure that my health was relatively good, so I made my appointment for the stress test. Alas, I arrived at the doctor's office, I came to find out that the appointments were running about a half an hour late. So I waited... and waited... and waited... that's what we do when we visit the doctor.

I've come to realize that when it comes to doctors' appointments – something most everyone experiences – we do a lot of waiting in life, sometimes for the good and sometimes for the bad. For a kid, waiting for opening the presents at Christmas seems an interminable amount of time; for me, I have the same problem with rush hour traffic (thank goodness my office is about one foot outside of my living quarters!).

Some people have a difficult time waiting for the things that are trivial, like grocery or fast food lines. Some people have a difficult time waiting for more serious issues in life. Last week, I visited a couple seniors at my parish who are getting up in years. Both individuals were extremely distraught in their respective situations – with their health declining and all of their family and friends gone from earth, they both shared with me their suffering of loneliness and the sadness that accompanied this long-experienced condition.

What do you say to people who are waiting to die? My stock response, my most sincere response which I very much believe, is that those in their senior years have the most important responsibility of praying for people like us who are in need of their prayers so that our lives can be drawn closer to the one who created us and the one who wishes to bring us home.

What do you say to a people who have lost all they have and all they are, as was the case in our first reading today? As Isaiah tried to comfort a Northern Kingdom of their horrendous loss at the hands of an Assyrian army and a warning to the Southern Kingdom of reforming their lives lest they fall in the same dilemma, so his words can easily apply to a people today that are more devoted to the things of earth than the things of heaven.

Today's gospel reminds us of a Chosen People who have been waiting for a Messiah to return, a political figure who would restore the land once lost some six centuries earlier. What John the Baptist professed instead was a different type of Messiah, one who would restore God's covenant with us in a spiritual way, in a more permanent way. When this Messiah came, when this Messiah had a disciple report to John the Baptist that the prophecy of the Old Testament had been fulfilled, we were not just taught about John's wonderful role as prophet and teacher of his age. What we also were taught was about a Messiah who infinitely was more important than St. John the Baptist.

The problem with waiting for Christmas is the same problem we experience at the fast food line, in rush hour traffic or even for the kids in the month of December – we are so much of a rush to get to the end of the story that we do not prepare sufficiently for that which we seek. We are taught in the faith that the lesson of waiting often corresponds with the lesson of preparing ourselves for that which is to come.

How often when we are in the fast food line or in rush hour traffic do we actually use that time for something constructive? How often in the world of faith do we use the time of Advent for praying and dedicating our lives to others in the same why that the Christ-child dedicated His life to us? My mother used to teach me about the value of a rosary in the grocery line or in the car, which was a beautiful way of taking those extra minutes God has given us to pray for souls who are looking for our help. Our Church teaches us that Advent is a time for confession, for prayer and for learning about the message of hope given to us by the Lord.

In Advent we get so caught up in the end game that we spend no time spiritually preparing ourselves for what is yet to come. We often find out that when we live this way, the spiritual part of Christmas can seem empty to us, like a good grade in class that was achieved without any work or a sporting award given to someone who cut corners in their preparation but truly not worthy of what was given.

Today's feast of *Gaudete Sunday* is an opportunity to recognize that waiting provides the benefit of preparing and that the time given to us by God is a time for reformation and reconciliation. I often think to myself that God gives me these extra days on earth to make right those things that I may have done wrong or could have done better. Possibly this is a time to realize that if we have faith, hope and Christian charity as the foundation of what we do, then the true gift of this Advent and Christmas Season is found in the way we invest ourselves for the sake of the poor, the downtrodden and those who cannot take care of themselves.

Let us realize that it is through this faith in God that we realize how much faith God has in us to reform our lives. Let us do so this Advent Season in the way we take this time of waiting to prepare ourselves well for what is yet to come. Let us teach our children well this lesson of faith and let us share this lesson of charity with the people that we meet. This is our prayer.

4th Sunday of Advent (Is 7: 10-14; Ps 24: 1-2, 3-4, 5-6; Rm 1: 1-7; Mt 1: 18-24)

The inspiration for today's homily comes from the shopping mall, the place that many of you have spent over the last few weeks, buying all those "Make Me Gag, Elmo" dolls which every child is asking to receive on the morning of December 25. As a priest, I love to go to the malls during the weekdays when everyone else is at work. It is at malls that the elderly walk the long corridors in order to get exercise in the early morning. It is at the malls that teens hang out at night in the video arcades and movie theatres.

The aspect of the mall that caught my attention this week is that "store directory" sign that you encounter when you walk into one of the mall's many entrances. When you enter a big complex with many stores, you need some direction in the manner you need to shop. Most importantly for me, I am in need of that little arrow that points me to the spot where I am standing, so that I can find my bearings within the building in which I stand.

In the world of faith, these signposts are essential to our journey, since without these markers, we would become lost. If we visit a mall on a constant basis, we don't need to look for directories; if we come to Mass on a regular basis, then our Lord becomes the sign that guides us and provides the bearings we need to find the path to heaven.

Today's readings point to one specific sign of faith that is so obvious to us that you would think we could not overlook it. It is a sign that gives us our bearing within this Advent Season. The sign is named *Emmanuel* - God is with us. The first reading points us to this Emmanuel who is given to Ahaz, this Emmanuel that becomes the title for King David's successor who will come to reclaim Jerusalem. Though the context of the reading refers to Ahaz's son as the successor to the Davidic line, we see that the word Emmanuel is a kingly title, one of honor and prestige.

This same word, Emmanuel, is used again by the angel of the Lord to this person Joseph, who is an heir to David's throne. The angel tells Joseph that the great Emmanuel will come through the power of the Holy Spirit through a virgin. Joseph ends up accepting this Emmanuel as His own son. Because of this, Emmanuel will be both the Son of God and by virtue of being Joseph's adopted son, a successor to the kingdom of David.

So we are now told everything: this Emmanuel is the Son of God, a king, a successor to David, the Lord most high. We have seen with our own eyes what Emmanuel has done for us. This Emmanuel is our salvation. The arrow points to our savior and there's a big sign flashing over Emmanuel's head like the Star of David. The sign becomes easy to see for those who strive to look for it.

The celebration of our Lord's nativity begins in the next week. How are we preparing for this celebration? How do we recognize this sign? At our parish (and I venture to say at most parishes), students from our school and religious education Programs write cards, wrap poinsettias and make rosaries for some of our homebound parishioners as well. Our confirmation students then take these gifts to the homebound parishioners who would otherwise have no one visiting them at Christmas and offer them the Spirit of Christ's presence at their homes, which are presented by the adults in our parish. Our adults invest in Christmas programs sponsored by our Food Pantry & St. Vincent de Paul Society. To prepare for Christmas spiritually, the good folks in our community spend so many hours in our Adoration Chapel, giving thanks to the Lord for the life yet to come, a life we commemorate each year by first anticipating the celebration with prayer and service and then celebrating the event through time spent with our Lord and family.

Whenever I have spent time with the kids on these Christmas projects, I become so moved by the faith of those that we visit that the immovable wreck known as your parish pastor can sometimes be brought to tears. A few years ago, I recall how one of our caroling groups visited a particular homebound man who was taking radiation treatments, thus not able to invite the students into his home. Instead, the kids sang carols outside the man's porch.

As the man heard the music, he cracked the door to listen to the carols and commented on how wonderful it was that someone visited. The man confided with us that because of his medical condition, very few people in his family wanted to spend time with him at Christmas. For him, the moment that the kids gave him *was* his Christmas. The man was so excited, he began to compliment everyone in the group and thanked them for making him smile.

During this Fourth Week of Advent, we seek this signpost of faith, this presence of our Emmanuel, by living the example of love and finding this sign of love in our hearts. We sing songs, put up the lights, get out the decorations and pray together. We remember those who have not experienced the love of Emmanuel and pray that God help them in their lives as well. We also remember that we ourselves still have a long way to go in being worthy of this gift and ask God to be with us during good times and bad.

As a conclusion to this homily, I offer you the words of Pope Leo the Great, who points us to this Emmanuel from within our hearts and the transformation that takes place within our hearts and our world for those who are led by this sign of the Christ-light. Pope Leo writes,

"(On Christmas), our Savior is born; let us rejoice. Sadness should have no place on this birthday of life. The fear of death has been swallowed up; life brings us joy with the promise of eternal happiness. No one is shut out from this joy; all share the same reason for rejoicing. Our Lord, victor over sin and death, finding no one (man) free from sin, came to free us all. Let the saints rejoice as they (he) see the palm of victory at hand. Let the sinners be glad as they receive the offer of forgiveness."[v]

Let us encounter this sign of Emmanuel's love in our faith. Let us become the window that allows this sign to shine forth. Let us share this sign with the people that we meet. This is our prayer.

Stories on the Journey: The Season of Christmas
(Cycle A Homilies)

The Solemnity of Christmas (The Incarnation of Our Lord)

I have been in a nostalgic mood as of late, as I ponder over the movies and songs of my younger days, wishing my cinematic youth could have begun in the 1940s and 50s and being present when the Christmas Classics like *White Christmas, Miracle on 34th Street* and *Going My Way* first graced our movie screens. The movies in and of themselves are somewhat dated in the modern age, but the sentiment of innocence in those movies remains strong to this day.

Take the movie "White Christmas," for example. It is not the best of the Christmas films, nor does it possess the best of plots ("Gee whiz, let's whip together a musical show in the barn to pay off the bills!"). But if you get invested in the musical numbers and listen to those wonderful songs penned by Irving Berlin, you can't help but be drawn into the sentiment of the holiday season.

For those who are practical, however, there is nothing practical about the beautiful "Winter Wonderland" about which we are singing. If you have to travel through the snow, you may not enjoy the blizzard-like conditions which stall traffic to a crawl. You may not enjoy the snow if you have to plow it, clean it off your cars or for the guy on the sleigh who has to deliver presents to the kids on Christmas Eve. Symbolically, though, to celebrate a literal White Christmas on December 24-25 fulfills the wishes of those wide-eyed innocent children who have been dreaming of this night for a good long time.

Rev. Peter G. Jankowski

I find great comfort in a White Christmas, spiritually speaking, because the image of the snow covering the cold ground of winter is reminiscent to me of Psalm 51, a prayer which we recite on the First Sunday of Lent which reminds us that our Lord *wants* to cover us with his love and protection, even though our sinful nature often prohibits the Lord from doing just that.

I love the words of the Psalm, because they are words of invitation for those who may have fallen away from the Church and are seeking a way back, words that tell us that God never wants to go away, that God always wants to fall upon us and make us clean. The Psalmist writes (vss. 9-15),

> Cleanse me with hyssop, that I may be pure;
> wash me and I will be whiter than snow.
> You will let me hear gladness and joy;
> the bones you have crushed will rejoice.
> Turn away your face from my sins;
> blot out all my iniquities.
> A clean heart create for me, God;
> renew within me a steadfast spirit.
> Do not drive me from before your face,
> nor take from me your holy spirit.
> Restore to me the gladness of your salvation;
> uphold me with a willing spirit.
> I will teach the wicked your ways,
> that sinners may return to you.[vi]

We encounter the image of snowfall over twenty times within the writings of scripture and the image of snow is often used as a symbol of cleansing and healing, especially during the worst of times. In the

Book of Job, for example, when the times seemed the darkest in life for our protagonist, Job implores the Lord to make him clean, to wash his soul with the snow of righteousness and love. Psalms 147 & 148 use the image of snow as a type of manner in which God's love is spread throughout the land, as if to say that no person or no culture is exempt from this love, for the snow that falls gently rests upon all of creation and all of creation finds the opportunity to be made anew. In the first chapter of the Book of the Prophet Isaiah, our hero implores the Chosen People to turn away from their scarlet ways and to embrace the Lord, who will cleanse their souls as if they were whiter than snow (Is 1: 18). In the Book of Daniel and from the Transfiguration story from the Gospel of Matthew, our Lord's appearance takes the form of being "whiter than snow," with the snow representing the type of holiness that we all strive to live (see Dan 7: 9; Mt 28: 3; Mk 9: 3; and Rev 1: 14).

To take this discussion further, I found a beautiful spiritual poem in my research that focuses on this particular theme, a poem written by St. Thérèse of Lisieux in her poem, "The Flower." For this beautiful Carmelite doctor of the Church who lived only twenty-four years on this earth, her image of what blooms forth from this "White Christmas" serves as the inspiration for why we come to pray at this solemnity in the first place, the image of the Lord coming forth for the purity of the world. St. Thérèse writes,

> All the earth with snow is covered,
> Everywhere the white frosts reign;
> Winter and his gloomy courtiers

Hold their court on earth again.
But for you has bloomed *the Flower*
Of the fields, who comes to earth
From the fatherland of heaven,
Where eternal spring has birth.
Near the Rose of Christmas, Sister!
In the lowly grasses hide,
And be like the humble flowerets,
Of heaven's King the lowly bride![vii]

I realize that St. Thérèse perceived snow as a type of negative in this poem, but in my reflection, I reflected on her poem, changing the snow symbolism of her poem to reflect that often found in the scriptures. I thought to myself that in the perspective of a loving winter, if we perceive the snow as a symbolic cleansing of the ground which makes all things clean with God, from the winter plains comes forth a rose that has no business growing in the freezing cold of winter. The woman described in the poem who is made clean becomes the vessel from which the rose shines forth and enters the world.

This interpretation of the poem serves as a good image for me – as St. Thérèse directs this prayer to our Blessed Mother, who serves as the bearer of this new flower of winter, so we, too, are given this particular image in 2010 to plant the seeds of faith in this white landscape to make this garden of faith grow as well.

The image of a White Christmas or a Winter Wonderland or us dashing through the snow in a one horse open sleigh very much reflects the life of innocence that covers us in this month of December and makes anew a life that might be burdened by the other months of the year. We come here to celebrate the flower of hope that comes through this winter covering and the innocence, if but for one day, that we seek to regain in a life filled with much turmoil.

As we begin this Christmas journey together, we are given the symbol of a newness of life that we should embrace with all our hearts. It may not be a great image for those who have to drive through it but for those who gaze upon it and watch the kids dancing upon it making their snow angels and men of white, we can't help but smile because we remind ourselves that God is still with us, that God came to live with us and that the possibility of salvation is made manifest by the child in that crib and the flower that grows from the land of white.

Please know you are all very much in our thoughts and prayers this Christmas Season. Please know we love you very much. Maybe today can be the day that we put all those things that separate us aside so that we can make ourselves anew on the inside as the land has been made anew on the outside. May your days be merry and bright and may all your Christmases be covered with the innocence of Christ, represented by the newly fallen snow and the child in the manger. Merry Christmas! This is our prayer.

Rev. Peter G. Jankowski

The Feast of the Holy Family (Sir 3: 3-7, 14-17a; Ps 128: 1-2, 3, 4-5; Col 3: 12-21 or 3: 12-17 (opt.); Mt 2: 13-15, 19-23)

As a pastor of this Church, I recently had an opportunity to celebrate a Christmas wedding service for a couple named Michael and Samantha. Michael would eventually receive the sacraments of Baptism, Confirmation and Eucharist for the first time at the Easter Vigil next year and the Church asks that he put his "ducks in a row" before he can receive these sacraments. So at 11:00 a.m. one Saturday morning, the family gathered to celebrate the sacrament of Marriage.

Present at the wedding were Michael and Sam's parents, friends and little baby girl who was one-year-old. Mike and Sam were really excited to share their love again, as witnessed by God and the community. I, too, was glad to see this event happen, since this particular weekend focuses on the celebration of the Holy Family, the gift of Mary, Joseph and the baby Jesus in our community.

I remember a couple years back at another wedding I celebrated at this time when instead of having the bride process towards the Blessed Mother for the "Ave Maria," that the couple wished to process instead towards the nativity set in order to ask for the Holy Family to impart their blessings on them. I think there is a great symbolism in such an act – in prayer, the couple is asking the Holy Family to assist another couple in holiness as well. The fact is, we all need to ask the same gift of Mary, Joseph and Jesus.

In 1988, St. Pope John Paul II preached about this gift of holiness in a homily given in Mbabane, Swaziland during an apostolic journey. In this homily, the pope preached that all Christian families are on a sacred mission in life, a mission to promote truth and respect within their households and within the Church itself. The pope told us that holiness begins with the love between a husband and wife, a love that is passed down to their children. If this love is fostered within the family, then we all can see the gift of the Trinity reflected within the family, a love of family members bonded by the spirit, in the same way as a Father and Son are bonded by the Spirit. It is through this mission that the Church is lived and passed on. It is through this mission that a family is made holy.[viii]

Today, fathers and mothers are challenged to be good role models for their children. They are encouraged to live out the gospel message by coming to church and teaching their kids about the faith. They are told that the best example of teaching the faith is by living the faith and by imitating the gift of Mary and Joseph, they show their children what unconditional love means. They remind us of a holy man name Joseph, who took in this woman Mary and her son and made them part of his life. They remind us of a mother Mary who accepted this son into her life under very difficult circumstances. By sharing their love, all couples in this room remind us about the love of parenthood, the love of Mary and Joseph.

Children are taught to listen to their parents, to give them respect and to learn from their example. If parents are living the gospel message, then the kids are able to carry that message within their own lives and share it with their own children. Children are taught to be respectful to their own brothers and sisters, to remember that everyone is a gift from God and to cherish their siblings is to cherish life.

I, as a priest, am given the responsibility of teaching you the gospel message as a steward and defender of the faith. People are called to listen and to respect the priest because of whom I represent and I am called to live the life of Christ because I have made a promise to do so. I am called to be a steward of the faith and you are called to follow the message that Christ preaches through me.

I have also learned as a priest that there are two families whom I serve and love: my biological family and my spiritual one. At the Christmas Masses, I made a point to thank my parents for their gift of love in my life. I also took time to thank all of you as well. It is my responsibility to serve you with all my heart, not as a token gesture but with everything I have. Christ did that for us; we are called to do the same for each other.

There is a point during the Mass when we give each other a sign of peace. This, too, is not meant as a token gesture but as a genuine sign of love that allows us to recognize each other as brothers and sisters. If we understand this, then we commit ourselves to welcoming those in this world and in this room as part of our family, as people that are considered special.

Thus, we come together both as biological families and spiritual ones, committed to following a mission of truth and love throughout the world. Let us not make this a token effort but a sincere sign of our dedication to the faith. May we be sacred as the Holy Family is sacred. May we treat each other with respect and love. This is how we grow in faith. This is our prayer today.

The Epiphany of the Lord (Is 60: 1-6; Ps 72: 1-2, 7-8, 10-11, 12-13; Eph 3: 2-3a, 5-6; Mt 2: 1-12)

> Besides the image of the star, which strikes upon the bodily eye, more brilliantly had the light of truth illuminated their hearts, leading them, even before they had set out, to prepare gifts that were befitting to his dignity; and this pertains to the illumination of faith.[ix]

I found this quotation from a homily once given by St. Pope Leo the Great some 1600 years ago during a time of great transition in the Church. As much political and theological turmoil rocked our Catholic belief system during this era of growth, Pope Leo masterfully kept Mother Church united in the faith and, most importantly, kept the faith accessible to the simple believer.

As we commemorate the visit of magi to our Lord this weekend in this Holy Feast of Epiphany, I was thinking about the differences in the way we celebrate Christmas through our senses and through our soul and how we make this faith accessible to the faithful of today's age. We are a sensual people – we like to experience the joys of a season or event like Christmas by seeing the decorations, by tasting the food, by feeling the falling snow, by touching the baby Jesus in the nativity, by smelling the fragrance of incense and by hearing the wonderful songs offered by our choirs. But as much as we enjoy the season through the senses, those experiences become fleeting ones at that – eventually those things that we sense go away and the experience becomes short-lived.

During my reflection this week, I started to wonder the manner in which the star of the East could become not just a vision for the eye but a light that could penetrate the heart (using the analogy given to us by St. Pope Leo), a light that would remain in our souls for the rest of our existence. I wondered to myself if this experience of faith, as wonderful as Christmas can make it alive, is as fleeting to us as the present season will come and go. It certainly has affected the attendance at our Masses – we are blessed to have all of you with us today but this number certainly does not compare to the ones that attended our Christmas Masses just eight days ago.

What does it mean to embrace the Christmas light? What does it mean to reject it? How can we hold on to that presence of Christ and that light of faith so that it remains meaningful throughout all our days on earth and beyond?

These last two weeks, I have encountered too many experiences in life and death and the manner in which the faithful have embraced the Christmas spirit. Over the last two weeks, I have celebrated eight funerals of eight individuals whose lives were vastly unique and very different from the other beloved deceased whose lives I remembered. Especially for me, the last two funerals I celebrated this week illustrated for me the pains of losing one's focus on the light and another whose light shined brightly in everything they did.

One of my funerals this last week was celebrated for a 20-year-old college-aged student named Jill, a young woman whose parents and family loved her very much and whose family offered her a Christian household with great care. Jill and her siblings attended our Religious Education classes – our teachers from that time fondly remembered Jill, her brother and sister and even attended last week's funeral in honor of the family. The kids did well at public school as well. While attending classes, Jill became skilled in the fine arts and in the process became proficient in playing the clarinet, the guitar and the piano. Jill's future path had great potential during her high school years.

Then one day, Jill lost the light. For whatever reason, this high school student turned to individuals who replaced the one true God with a fleeting addition that haunted her for the rest of her life. As I teach parents whose children suffer these types of addictions, we all need to realize that, at first, the investment into drugs, alcohol, gambling or sex outside of marriage is very sinful indeed; if treated in its early stages, the sin can be overcome with a good deal of help. But when the sin moves into more advanced stages, the addicted person no longer has control of their senses; by that time, the addiction has then taken control. In this state, you no longer speak to the person – you speak to the addiction. In the case of Jill, the addiction took her life prematurely.

As with many times within my life, I usually end up with a loss of words as to what I need to say to a family that grieves in these situations. Sometimes the best thing to say is nothing at all and just be present for those who grieve. The mother in this case was the pillar of strength for those who surrounded her and I was in awe of her being able to keep herself together in the most difficult of times. I ask you to pray for Jill and to pray for the family. They told me that they still pray for Jill and try to help her during the next phase of your spiritual journey.

The second story is much more positive. As Jill died at the young age of 20, a woman named Mary also passed away last week after spending 73 beautiful years on this earth. For those of you who do not know Mary, she lived only a couple of blocks away from the parish and was noted for the bountiful garden that she grew at the corner of her property with all kinds of produce that she would cook for her 5:00 dinner each day for the husband and family. Mary was a stay at home mom – her children attended St. Pat's School. She came to all the basketball games, she was part of the Mother's Club at the parish and she would always give one of the former pastors here at the parish a piece of advice along the way, being one of those pillars of faith who liked to offer her two cents to the pastor at the time.

However, the contribution of Mary's family to this parish goes well beyond garden vegetables and is quite significant to us in these pews, as their contribution literally has provided a roof over our heads. If you know a little history about our parish, Mary's great-grandfather was one Charles Wallace, the architect who supervised the construction of this building inside which we are celebrating our Sunday liturgy today. In 1919, Charles Wallace actually built two identical churches simultaneously in the Joliet area, one mile apart from each other: St. Patrick's Church here on Marion Street and St. Raymond's Church one-mile north of us. Some thirty years later in 1950, the powers that be established a diocese seated here in Joliet and decided to "ugly up" St. Ray's so that they could call that building a cathedral. In its heart, though, St. Ray's and St. Pat's are brick relatives to each other and for the gift of the Wallace family, we all give great thanks.

Mary Wallace-Addams served for us as a bridge that connected the history of this parish community to the present. As she carried on the Christian tradition of her heritage, so we remind ourselves of the number of individuals who worked very hard to build these walls so that we could pray together. The Wallace Family BUILT this church and then they PRAYED in this church. They set the example, SHE set the example and both the Wallace and Addams families showed us the manner by which we shine this light of faith.

How do we set this example of faith in today's age? How do we allow the light to penetrate our hearts? I asked myself if Charles Wallace would have approved of us building that chapel on the corner of our property and I think he would have approved of the addition because it serves as an extension to the light that already exists at the parish. I would hope that the life of faith we have built these last 173 years has been a good testimony to what St. Patrick's Church has held to believe for the communities she has served.

We have prayed for those like Jill who have lost the light and ask God to show her the way. We give thanks for those like Mary whose family has shown us the light in the example of faith they have presented to us. It is the same light to which our Lord introduced us at baptism. It is the same light that was sealed within us at Confirmation. It is the same light that led the magi to the Lord some two thousand years ago. It is the same light that we commemorate today.

If we are to honor the memories of the faithful that have come before us, we must dedicate ourselves to follow the words of Pope Leo and allow the light of this feast to penetrate our hearts. We must not allow the light to be something fleeting to our senses but essential to our souls and our hearts. For when we continue to serve the poor, comfort those who grieve and pray for those in need, we share the light in the same way Christ shared in while he walked the earth. We become the lamps that light the world and unite the faithful in love.

May this light lead us to where we need to go and may we shine this light upon the people that we meet. This is our prayer.

The Baptism of the Lord (Is 42: 1-4, 6-7; Ps 29: 1-2, 3-4, 3b-9b-10; Acts 10: 34-38; Mt 3: 13-17)

As we mark the last weekend of the Christmas Season with this Mass commemorating the Lord's Baptism, I was inspired this week by a conversation with a faithful member of our parish who I will call "John." At this meeting sat a good-hearted man who dedicated his life taking care of his wife and children. John lived a good married life without any negligible problems. His children were raised well, they graduated from college with good grades and then established themselves as wonderful contributors in our society. John and his wife have been happily married for over three decades and have been involved in all the things that God and God's Church would ask of them to do for the sake of the kingdom. On the surface, all seemed well in the family and all seemed well for John himself.

That said, John visited me last week to confront a few spiritual matters he has recently encountered, the types of questions that I have heard numerous times in my priesthood: Now that my kids have left home, what is next for me to do? What is my purpose in life? Have I done enough to get to heaven? Why do I feel like my life and my faith are so repetitious and sometimes without meaning?

I struggle mightily with these questions because these questions are posed to me this time of year more than any other. During Christmastime after you get through the joy of opening presents, many in our society ask themselves "what is next?" At times, we often think that the "joy" of Christmas disappears once that last gift is opened, as if the season magically disappears with that one tradition. I have noticed more and more that family time around the table often gets suppressed on Christmas Day by those who will go out to movie theaters or places of entertainment that get more crowded each year, as the need to find new and exciting ways to celebrate Christmas each year seems to be of great need among this era's society.

Now there is nothing wrong with going to the movies or even going out for a drive on Christmas Day if this is what a family wishes to do. However, in my mind, John is asking me more about the substance of life rather than the temporary pleasures that our world provides, pleasures that ultimately lose their value as soon as they are consumed. In my reflection, John was seeking answers concerning what the "core" of the Christmas Season and life are all about, a "core" that becomes somewhat of an afterthought in a society that often jumps from one fleeting moment to another.

I think John posed these questions to me because he has entered a transitional point of his life where he has been trying to reconnect with the "core" that has woven itself through everything he has done up to this point. John was asking me questions that people most often ask when their kids have left the home and the married couple have entered the next phase in their life's journey. In these cases, adjustments in life need to be made by the married couple, who return back to the childless state in which they first started their marriage.

As with all seasons in our liturgical year, as with all facets of our Christian life, I have come to the realization that these moments of joy find their greatest meaning when we put work into understanding the meaning of what these events have for us in life and how they fit into God's plan of salvation. In order to make a house look nice and pretty, you actually have to spend time putting all those lights up, knowing that at the end of the season you have to take them right back down. As I look at this beautifully decorated church, I think to myself about the amount of time it took the people to put up the trimmings and the effort it takes to maintain what the people have decorated. In the world of faith or in the world of a marriage or religious vocation, the amount of time we dedicate to our spouse of our Church deepens our love for the person to whom we dedicate ourselves and as a result, everything seemingly fits into the purpose of our Christian life and thus our lives achieve a greater meaning.

That is the problem with life, of course – life requires *work* and it requires *perseverance*. It is a rare thing in secular life that a person has goodness just fall on their lap – goodness most often is achieved in life by the person who chooses to live this life and works hard to allow this goodness to shine forth. This church did not appear decorated magically – a group of faithful parishioners spent a great deal of time planning how to put up the flowers and trees because the decorations heighten the Christmas experience of faith. The same applies to a good marriage or a good vocation – 10% of our effort comes out of love for what we do and the other 90% comes from hard work. If you honestly talk to any married couple about the choice of their vocation, they will tell you how difficult it is to worry about their children or the well-being of their spouse on a daily basis. Yes, the end result of our vocations or of our faith life comes from our efforts that pave the way for the goodness of God to shine forth.

The Feast of the Lord's Baptism serves as a bridge between the Season of Light and the Season in Ordinary Time. In my vision of the faith, I see this feast as the bridge between celebration and hard work. Everyone likes to celebrate Christmas – very few like to spend all that time putting up the lights or cleaning the kitchen after the huge family Christmas dinner. However, as we learn from the lessons of our Sacred Scripture, it is Jesus' ministry that begins at his own baptism that paves the way for the work is about to do and makes meaningful the death and resurrection that is yet to come. If you understand your purpose in life, then every Christian activity between your baptism and your calling to the Lord at the end of life makes sense because those actions become part of the plan that God has chosen you to live.

Some people might wonder why Jesus would endure such laborious work for our sake, since his own purpose for existence is fulfilled in heaven. Since is God, this Christ could have easily enjoyed the eternal rest that one can find in the kingdom of heaven. In fact, John the Baptist in today's reading even questions why our Lord would <u>need</u> to be baptized in preparation for his ministry – the fact is, Jesus does not need to be baptized, does not need to serve or work. Jesus is the only person in the history of creation that does <u>not</u> need to work for a living and yet still is baptized in the Jordan by John the Baptist. Why?

The answer to this question sets the model and example for us to understand the kind of effort we need to accomplish in this world in order for us to find this eternal rest to heaven as well. As an adult teaches the child through their example of life, so this Christ teaches us how to find God through His. It is through His example of baptism that we learn about the gift of the water and new life. It is through His example of serving the poor and the needy that we learn to do the same. It is through His dying on the cross that we learn to sacrifice our own lives, even to the death, for the salvation of those around us.

In my reflection, Christ lives and dies on earth because chooses to care about our lives more than we even do. cares more about our lives than cares about His own. For this reason, we understand why this Mass is so important – it's an act of love that we cannot comprehend fully, but we come to Mass to learn about this love so that we can embrace it and then model it for others.

The example that this Jesus the Christ sets forth for us is the lesson of humility that is the key theme that influences all of our liturgical seasons. By entering the world in a manger, our Lord humbly enters an existence that welcomes both the poor and the rich, an existence worthy of both shepherds and kings. By becoming baptized, our Lord humbles Himself to someone else, someone lesser, presenting Himself not as a king that rules or even as an equal but rather as a servant who is willing to bend to His knee to be washed in the waters of baptism by another and then to wash the feet of those could easily raise or destroy. The example that our Lord sets for us in Matthew's gospel is one that is often embraced by the outsider but taken for granted by those in the Gospel that become too comfortable in their own interpretation of the faith that they choose not to learn about the ways that God has set forth for them.

The last line that concludes this Mass and begins our new liturgical season becomes especially important to us, since those words commission us to go out and do the work of the Lord in the world, following the example that our Lord set for us. I guess my response to John is that, after "loving and serving the Lord" these many years, giving themselves to both the Church and to their families, I would like to think that "what is next" is to enjoy the fruits of one's labors and to give thanks to the spouses, kids and grandkids that have become part of our lives. I guess my response to John is that coming to Mass allows us to give thanks to God for all the blessings in life his family has been given. We probably realize that as our lives have evolved, our talents have evolved as well, as we probably have become more adept at some talents in life and probably have become less adept in others.

If we follow St. Paul's admonition to do whatever we do, in word or in work, to do it in the name of the Lord (Colossians 3: 17), then we realize that what we do on a daily basis may be monotonous to some, but is considered a building block of faith to God. It is these building blocks that make a kingdom so let us build this kingdom well.

Let us follow the example that Christ has given us by first embracing the baptismal promises we made and continue to make with God. As we celebrate this bridge that connects the Season of Christmas to Ordinary Time, let us all follow the example of Christ's mission on earth and model the type of Christian work that is necessary to achieve salvation. Let us offer the work of love to the people that we meet. That is how we answer the questions concerning the purpose of our life. This is our prayer.

Stories on the Journey:
The Season of Lent
& Holy Week
(Cycle A Homilies)

Rev. Peter G. Jankowski

Ash Wednesday (Joel 2: 1-2,12-17 or Isaiah 58: 1-12 2 Corinthians 5: 20b-6: 10 Matthew 6: 1-6,16-21)

Last year at the end of the Season of Lent, we began Holy Week by passing out palms to the people who came to Mass. The symbolism of the palms was important; as the faithful people of the first century waved them in Jerusalem during Jesus' triumphal entry into the city, so we reenact the same tradition by waving our palms and crying out, "Hosanna in the Highest! Blessed is he who comes in the name of the Lord!" At the beginning of the holiest week of the year, we commemorate our Lord's jubilant entry into Jerusalem, working our way to the Passion reading, which retells how a once jubilant people turn against our Lord on Good Friday. Yet, our Lord's death truly is a *Good* Friday, not because the Lord dies but because dies for the sake of our sinful human condition, only to be raised up at Easter, paving the way for the salvation that waits for those who follow His example.

At the end of the Palm Sunday service each year, we invite the faithful to take their palms home with them. We even sponsor "palm braiding" classes for those who wish to make fancy designs from the palms given to them. With fancy design in hand, we invite the faithful to place their palms in a location that would remind them of their dependence on Christ in their lives. Up until a few weeks ago, the people consented and did just that.

As is tradition, though, we often ask people to return their dried palms to church prior to this particular Mass so that we can use them in the making of ashes. When we gathered all these palms, we place them in a container and burn them. We sift the ashes from the remaining pieces of palm (because we don't want to stick "chunks" on anyone's forehead). As we start the Lenten Season the following year, we use the same symbol that ended the previous year's Lenten Season, used in a different fashion.

We use these ashes to remind the faithful that if God is the center of our life then all things are possible. We are reminded if God is not the center of our life, we are nothing; we return to dust and ash. The lines that we used in this rite of ashes, *Remember you are dust and unto dust you shall return* remind us of the necessary role God plays in our lives.

We are reminded that Christ had to carry the weight of sin on His shoulders so that we could be saved. We are reminded that Christ took time from heaven to be with us in this imperfect world; sacrificed His life so that we could save ours. In return, God asks us during these 40 days to give back as well, to sacrifice a little so that we can remember how much sacrificed for us.

During this season of Lent, we will be asked to give up something – whether it is TV or candy or whatever it might be – and to take the time that we would normally indulge in luxury to put it towards Christ and love. We are taught that in Lent we need to focus on prayer, fasting and almsgiving, the three penances that make us think about Christ's sacrifice in our lives.

As we receive these ashes, let us focus on our dependence for God. Let us learn to sacrifice as sacrificed for us. Let us share this message and carry it within our hearts for these 40 days. This is our prayer.

1st Sunday of Lent (Gen 2: 7-9; 3: 1-7; Ps 51: 3-4, 5-6, 12-13, 14-17; Rm 5: 12-19 or 5: 12, 17-19; Mt 4: 1-11)

During my third year in upper graduate seminary, I had the privilege of living with two seminarians who were studying for the Archdiocese of Beijing, China. Both students were sent to the United States as part of an agreement that was made between the official, government-sanctioned church in China and the Spirit-guided Church in Vatican City. The deal that was negotiated was that some of the Chinese seminarians were given permission to study their theology in Roman Catholic institutions and, in return, the Chinese government would loosen their grip on the priests from the underground church who were unjustly imprisoned and mistreated because of the allegiance they held to the universal Catholic Church. Let's name the two students' names "John" & "James."

Neither John nor James spoke any English when they first arrived in the states. John was more diligent in his studies; James seemed to adapt more to the "social customs" of his new country without worrying too much about the education that went with it. I was asked to take John under my wing and tutor him about the ways of the faith and, in the friendship that grew from that relationship, John taught me about the difference between those who served in the government-sanctioned Church versus what is often called "the underground Church." John told me that the path of those in the underground Church is quite difficult, that this life might lead someone to prison or much worse.

With these comments, John made me reflect intensely on the word of God and the path that each of us is called to take towards this kingdom of heaven. As we gather at this Mass to pray together, I am certain that each of us has our challenges in life that we must overcome and temptations to take the easy way out of the challenges which we face. The challenges might be simple ones: to go on a diet, how to manage our finances, or which candidate to select for public office. Some challenges might seem more difficult: how to stay faithful in our respective vocations or how to love another person when that other person has wronged us in some way. For some, the easy challenges are hard and the harder challenges are easy. For some, the phrase "lead us not into temptation" might seem as lip service rather than something that someone should take to heart.

I have learned the hard way in life that following the will of God is a whole lot harder than following the will of society – society has a much different plan in life than God does. The old joke that is used in the life of ministry is that if you want to make God laugh, tell Him *your* plans in life. Society has plans for us in this world and those plans usually are hedonistic by nature. God has one plan for us – to get us to heaven. has given us the tools to achieve this goal; has given us His Son to show us the way. All we have to do is hold on to Christ and to follow the blueprint for salvation has set for us in the Bible and the teachings of the Church – all we are called to do is hold on for the ride and allow Christ to steer this boat and to carry us to the other side.

As we celebrate this first Sunday of Lent, I was thinking about how John taught me about the manner in which the Chinese faithful were directed to follow the will of God, the faithful were being pulled to remain obedient in two different directions – by the government and by the Church. On this first Sunday of Lent I recalled the story of one of John's fellow clergymen, Cardinal Ignatius Jung, who served 30 years in prison and another decade under house arrest on account of his adherence to the same faith that was called by God to live and punished by a government as a result of this adherence to the faith. As we read this story of Jesus' temptation in the desert, I began to think about the significant temptations in life that won't just make us gain a few points or save us a few dollars. I think about the temptations that can lead us to death. For the sake of Cardinal Jung, for the sake of the Chinese seminarians (especially James and John) I pray that each of us in this holy place are able to say with conviction the same words that serve the basis for their lives: "thy will be done" and "lead us not into temptation."

The fact is, to follow the will of God leads us all to the desert in order to fight off the temptations of life. This season of Lent reminds us how much easier life becomes when we succumb to sin and avoid the world of grace. The British scholar C. S. Lewis once wrote that the life of sin is like an easy, gentle path that provides little resistance and before you know it, you do not even realize that you have taken the path to hell until it seems too late. Sometimes this path to hell seems innocuous – cheating on a test, cheating on your vocation or cheating on the world becomes simple or complex temptations that slowly draw us away from the Lord. The small sins grow into large sins; the large sins demonstrate to God that we would rather live apart from Him than with Him. The fact is, if someone offers a person the easy way to life with a little sin involved, the person will probably choose that life over the one that is full of grace but accompanied by suffering as well.

In the scripture readings, we understand the parallel between these lives of the profane and the sacred through the strength of obedience found in the persons of Adam and Christ. Both were given the challenge to follow the will of God in order to maintain this relationship. But as we are told in our first two readings today, Adam was tested by the devil and, as a result, Adam was lured away from this perfect relationship. Where Adam failed, Christ persevered. Where Adam succumbed to the temptation of sin, Christ remained obedient to God, right through the cross. We are told that if we follow the path of Christ and follow the will of the Father, our path will not be easy – it is very difficult to swim upstream in this life of society. The path of this life will eventually lead us to this cross that becomes a symbol of our faith life and a symbol of the type of service our Lord was willing to endure for us. However, the path of Christ carries us through the profane into the existence of perfection. The path set forth by Adam sets us on the nice easy slope to extinction.

I wish to conclude my homily today with a somewhat lengthy meditation from a man named

Rev. Peter G. Jankowski

Walter Ciszek, a Jesuit priest who spent 23 years in a Soviet prison after being convicted for supposedly spying on Russia as a "Vatican spy." Prior to his death in 1984, Fr. Ciszek wrote about the reason chose to accept the path that God asked of him and why, as a result, accepted the imprisonment that accompanied this path. For me, I read this reflection and realize that my struggles in life, though very important and significant to me, are extremely trivial in comparison to others. In the larger picture, the sufferings of others like Cardinal Ignatius Jung, Fr. Joseph Zong and Fr. Walter Ciszek serve as an inspiration for me during the Season of Lent to be more diligent in following the path that God has set for me. This reflection serves as my inspiration to follow God's will. This is what Fr. Ciszek writes:

> Choosing to do God's will and experiencing the spiritual freedom that followed was my greatest joy and the source of tremendous interior strength. For to know that directed me in all my actions, that sustained me with his grace, gave me a sense of peace and courage beyond description. Even in moments of human discouragement, the consciousness that I was fulfilling God's will in all that happened to me would serve to dispel all doubt and desolation. Whatever the trials of the moment, whatever the hardships or sufferings, more important than all these was the knowledge that they had been sent by God and served His divine providence. I could not always fathom the depths of His providence or pretend to understand His wisdom, but I was secure in the knowledge that

by abandoning myself to His will I was doing as perfectly as I could His will for me.

Spiritual freedom of this sort, as I knew from bitter experience, is not something that can be attained overnight or ever possessed in its final form. Every new day, every new hour of every day, every new circumstance and situation, every new act is a new opportunity to exercise this freedom. What is required for growth is an attitude of acceptance and openness to the will of God, rather than some planned approach or calculated method. Even ascetical practices such as penances, fasting, or mortifications can be hindrances rather than helps if they are self-imposed. Striving instead to eliminate all self-will, to accept God's will revealed in the circumstances of daily life, is the surest way to achieve growth in conformity to the will of God. It will provide more than enough virtue to be practiced, suffering to be sustained, pain to be borne; more importantly still, it will make us fit instruments to achieve His designs, not only for our own salvation but for others as well. The service of God must take preference over all else.[x]

For the sake of Fr. John & James, Cardinal Jung and Fr. Walter, may we learn to follow God's will and seek the path of spiritual freedom that comes from this obedience. This is our prayer.

2nd Sunday of Lent (Gen 12: 1-4a; Ps 33: 4-5, 18-19, 20-22; 2 Tim 1: 8b-10; Mt 17: 1-9)

Every Second Sunday of Lent, the theme of our gospel reading focuses on the transfiguration of our Lord, the moment when Jesus climbs a mountain with His disciples and reveals Himself to be the Christ, whom Peter acknowledged as such in the preceding chapter of Matthew the beloved Son of our Father, the one who was sent to fulfill the law and the prophesies of the Old Testament. All three gospels tell us that on this mountain, on this peak which symbolizes the greatest location on earth to encounter the divine, both Moses and Elijah appeared, Moses representing the law of the faith and Elijah representing prophetic discourse. The gospels essentially tell us that Jesus is the new law and the new prophet, the one who fulfills all that the law and the prophets have discussed from the past and makes real in the present.

Where the three gospels differ significantly concerns the disposition of the three disciples to whom the Lord reveals Himself. The Gospel of Mark portrays the disciples as clueless to the meaning of this Transfiguration, a theme that weaves itself throughout the entire Markan text. The Gospel of Luke presents the disciples as having some type of divine, visionary dream from which the Lord awakens them. What the gospel of Matthew does, in contradistinction to the gospels of Mark and Luke, is to portray the disciples as fully awake and fully cognizant of the divine presence that they have encountered and as a result, becoming scared out of their minds from what they encountered.

I don't think that this response is so unique from the type of response any one of us would have. Whenever any of us encounter something that is devastating or beatific, we all begin to shake and tremble. It amazes me that people in this world try to beat their chests and cry out with great bravado about their strength and resolve they have in the world, a resolve I interpret in the Catholic faith as some type of "Rambo theology." It amazes me how people believe that they can endure anything that is set before them, from small events in the world like a test or an important presentation at work to something much more serious such as a tsunami or some other type of natural disaster or unnatural war. The fact is, no matter how much we thump our chests concerning our strength in front of the divine, the presence of God that is revealed before us should and most likely will, scare the life out of us.

What our beloved Lord provides for us in this particular gospel reading and within the life of the faithful believer, is the means by which we may encounter the divine face-to-face without being afraid. It is the Lord who takes us by the hand and guides us to safety, the Lord who offers us the hand of love so that we can bond with Him during good times and in bad. It is our Lord who touched the disciples in today's gospel and gently instructed them not to be fearful, for with the Lord by their side they would be safe and sound; they would not fear the Lord for the Lord is the one who guides them to the place where they needed to go.

Two thousand years later, we realize that when we hold the hand of the Lord, it is who guides us through the desert of temptation in this Season of

Lent and up the mountain of faith. It is our Lord that guides us to the woman at the well and to the tomb of Lazarus. It is the Lord who guides us to the altar and through the cross and it is the Lord that tells us not to fear, for through the Lord's guidance that we find hope in the everlasting life rather than the fear we experience with the unknown that awaits us in the world yet to come.

As I reflected on the story of this transfigured Lord in Matthew's Gospel, I recalled the words of St. Pope John Paul II, who wrote about this event in an Apostolic Exhortation from 1986 entitled, "The Consecrated Life" *(Vita Consacrata)*. In this document, he instructs us that this moment of the Transfiguration was given to the disciples to prepare them for the sufferings and difficulties which they were to face in their ministry. The Holy Father writes that this image of Christ transfigured provided the disciples with enough strength to continue the difficult ministry that awaited them, as well as us in today's society. The only way to encounter and overcome these difficulties result from our dependence on God and our ability to reach out to the Lord in order to allow our Lord to guide us through these difficulties. It is these words of our Holy Father with which I wish to conclude today's homily. Our Holy Father writes,

> ... the disciples who have enjoyed this intimacy with the Master, surrounded for a moment by the splendor of the Trinitarian life and of the communion of saints and as it were caught up in the horizon of eternity, are immediately brought back to daily reality, where they see "Jesus only,"

in the lowliness of His human nature and are invited to return to the valley, to share with Him the toil of God's plan and to set off courageously on the way of the cross.

... The event of the Transfiguration marks a decisive moment in the ministry of Jesus. It is a revelatory event which strengthens the faith in the disciples' hearts, prepares them for the tragedy of the cross and prefigures the glory of the resurrection. This mystery is constantly relived by the Church, the people on its way to the eschatological encounter with its Lord.[xi]

May we find the presence of the divine spirit, revealed in our hearts, so that we may find the strength to encounter the challenges that await us, both in the season of Lent and within our life's journey. This is the manner in which the Lord wishes to show us we are loved and are safe. This is our prayer.

3rd Sunday of Lent (Ex 17: 3-7; Ps 95: 1-2, 6-7b, 7c-9; Rm 5: 1-2, 5-8; John 4: 5-42 or 4: 5-15, 19b-26, 39a, 40-42)

A few years ago, I was serving as Associate Pastor at St. Joseph's Parish in Addison, Illinois where the inspiration for today's homily took place. The city of Addison basically is divided into two sections: the more affluent section on the west side of town and the middle to lower class section on the east side, where I served. The people of St. Joe's are great –

people are great wherever you serve. But the people are poor nevertheless and the parish offered a social justice activity for the people who attended this Lenten event.

What intrigued me most about this event concerned the meal that was served to start that particular evening. Each person that entered the dining room was given a sticker, colored green, yellow or red (I told people that the stickers corresponded to one's looks: green represented good-looking, yellow represented so-so and red... naturally, I was wearing a green sticker). After the opening prayer, the student volunteers shared a meal with all who attended the event in a spirit of service. There was one sticking point to the meal, though: the people with the green stickers were served first, with a first class meal. As the faithful with the green stickers were being served, everyone else holding yellow and red stickers were salivating, waiting for their meals to arrive, only to find out that the people holding yellow stickers were served rice or oatmeal and juice, while those with the red stickers were served bread and water.

Naturally, there were many people in the room that were not happy. "I did not know that we were not all getting the same thing," they started to grumble. I noticed some people switching stickers, claiming that they were not served the proper food. I noticed that some parents with the green stickers were giving their portion of food to their kids who had the yellow or the red. At the end of the meal, some people understood the lesson that was given and many did not like the lesson while most of the kids themselves were waiting for the end of the day in order to rush off to McDonald's to get some dinner.

As I reflected on this event, I turned to our first reading from Exodus, a story that took place during the chosen people's forty years in the wilderness, protected by the Lord yet in search of a land that God promised to give them. If you look at the structure of the first five books of the Old Testament, the Book of Genesis generally covers around 2400 years, the Book of Exodus covers the one year the chosen people spent at Mt. Sinai, Leviticus is covered in what we might call "real time," and Numbers spans the great deal of the forty years in the wilderness. The last book of the Pentateuch, the Book of Deuteronomy, generally covers the last day of the life of Moses.

It is in those forty years of wandering that the sentiments of the chosen people very much paralleled the grumblings that I experienced at this social justice event in Addison, Illinois. In the story of this Exodus, God promised the chosen people that He would take care of them. What the people didn't realize was that the manner that God was to take care of them wasn't in the form of steak and eggs but in the form of manna and water. Manna was a type of frost that settled on the vegetation each night, hardening into a type of bread that was sufficient to eat. In today's story, we learn how God also provided water to the people in order to quench their thirst.

The fact was, though, that the people wanted more. For those wandering in the wilderness, it wasn't sufficient enough for them just to be fed; they wanted to live the high life. They did not want just bread and water; they wanted meals like the ones they were accustomed to eating before the Exodus. The fact was that the people's direction was led more by their stomachs than by their Lord, a violation of the First Commandment, a lapse in judgment that is evident in our society today concerning what was really important in life.

The story in our gospel reading takes this theme of feeding the needy and reverses the role of God and man. In our gospel story, it is God that wishes to be fed by us, as opposed to man being fed by God. Yet remarkably, the Samaritan woman's response of distrust echoes the same theme as questioned by the chosen people of the Old Testament: if this God is truly the God of all created things, why does God not treat us in the way that we see fit?

That same theme addressed by the chosen people, as well as the Samaritan woman, is the theme of today's homily, a phrase which I humorously recall in the old Wendy's Hamburgers commercial from years past: *Where's the beef?* When are you going to serve us in a manner fitting to us? For those who have no food, the question is a constant mantra to God. For those who have food, the question is amended: why haven't you provided us with more?

The theme of this activity at St. Joseph's Church was that some people in the world are in great need and it is the responsibility of those who have to support those who have not, in the same way that the love of God pours forth on those who seek this love. The food and love may not be what we exactly desire, but there is more food and love and charity of God to share, with plenty left over.

The fact is that 90% of all land in all third world countries is owned by 10% of the population. The fact is that the people who possess the greatest amount are often reluctant to share their gifts with others out of fear of losing what they already have. If we have learned nothing else from our gospel message, we have learned that God does not feed us with what we want – God gives us everything that we need, His heart and soul and calls us not to focus on the needs and desires of our stomach or eyes, but on the presence of the divine in our hearts. For when we do, when we put the needs of others ahead of our own needs, then the message of feeding those who are in need becomes not just a nice thing that we offer from our financial surplus, but an action that reflects our entire heart given to God in the same way that God's sacred heart is offered to us on the cross.

Next week marks the halfway point of the Lenten Season. Already I have heard grumblings from the kids about all the sacrifices that they have had to make this particular liturgical season. All of us are called to relive a penitential life through the disciplines of prayer, fasting and almsgiving. Of all the ways we can do this, perhaps in some small way we can express this penitential life by continuing to support the service ministries that we sponsor here at the parish. When we feed others, we feed our Lord. When we feed our Lord, what feeds us back is more than we can ever imagine. As stated in the twenty-fifth chapter of Matthew's gospel, when we serve the least of God's children, we serve God as well. Let us take this message to seeing the presence of God in the hearts of those whom we serve and by feeding our God through feeding and loving them. This is our prayer.

4th Sunday of Lent (1 Sam 16: 1b, 6-7, 10-13a; Ps 23: 1-3a, 3b-4, 5, 6; Eph 5: 8-14; John 9: 1-41 or 9: 1, 6-9, 13-17, 34-38)

My homily this weekend is inspired by the maintenance man and his contribution to our sacrament planning books that we hand out to all families wishing to have special Masses at our parish. The insertion reads as such...

- To prevent damage to the pews and other surfaces in the church, we ask that nothing be attached with tape, sticky tack, push tacks, glue, wire or paperclips.
- No balloons, butterflies or any other type of flying object may be stored or used in church or the vestibule.

As with most rules in life, guidelines like the ones I have read come as a result of abuses that have taken place at the church. As I have been told that our carpeting is now fourteen years old and is now bubbling up and rolling with any funeral casket that proceeds down the aisle, I have been asked to make sure we do what we can to protect our flooring until we find some resources to replace the carpet.

My favorite rule that I have been asked to enforce concerns the use of glitter in the church. I never thought I would be talking about glitter in a homily but my maintenance personnel have asked me to charge any couple that decides to drop what they call "a glitter bomb" inside the church. I am told that a "glitter bomb" is devised by florists who like to apply somewhat liberally as much glitter as possible to the plants they bring into church so that, as soon as the plants shake, the glitter shakes into the air, forms a dark cloud in the church which evenly showers down this shiny material into every crevice of the carpeting that one can find. To use the vernacular of those who clean our church, "You try to clean this place when a glitter bomb goes off and you'll understand why we have to call the carpet cleaners every week!" Poor, poor maintenance personnel...

Our church cleaners have gone so far as to request that when we replace the carpeting in the church that we tile underneath the pews so that he can better clean that dirt and mud that is tracked into church. Jim and his minions have gone so far as to provide us with special tile samples to show the community what needs to be purchased to protect our floor that will not need to be shampooed on a constant basis.

Their problem, of course, is that they are thinking like an adult rather than enjoying life like a kid. Whereas parents and maintenance men constantly become frustrated over those dirty substances that ruin a nicely cleaned floor, let's be honest, kids like to play in the mud! Didn't you like it when you were young? Didn't you like making mud pies and getting all messy with the mud, having fun with your friends and just having a good time? Didn't you like it when you finish having fun with your friends and then come into the house, tracking the mud into your house? Then your mother would see you all messed up and then pulls you out of your clothes, drags you to the bathtub and then washes you down until every last moist crumb of dirt is cleaned from your ears. For you younger tykes in our congregation, don't listen to Fr. Pete – listen to your parents and don't track mud into the house... even if it is fun to play in the mud!

You ever notice that sin is like playing in the mud? At first, we might get a little guilty making a mess, but the more you start playing, the more fun it starts to get. Eventually, you don't even think about what other people are going to think when you get back in the house. It's too much fun playing in the mud – you'll worry about the consequences later in life. The problem is, once you start playing in the mud, you might not ever want to stop. You might not realize how much of a mess it is going to make. Unless someone actually <u>does</u> stop you, you'll keep doing it until you either get caught or until kingdom come. It's a dangerous life to lead, this playing in the mud, but when you get stuck in the mud, it's almost impossible to get out.

I actually found a quotation attributed to our own St. Patrick of Ireland on this very subject that is on point with the homily I am preaching thus far. St. Patrick once said,

> Before I was humiliated I was like a stone that lies in deep mud and he who is mighty came and in His compassion raised me up and exalted me very high and placed me on the top of the wall.[xii]

So if we went down this path, we can see mud as a parallel to sin, which plays itself out quite often in the scriptures. In the case of today's gospel, though, the symbolism of mud is taken quite differently in the first century than we take it now. For us, saliva and mud are considered unclean substances which we should avoid as much as possible for obvious reasons. However, in first century Judaism, saliva and mud were considered holistic medicine and was often used in the curing of those who were sick. For Christ to wet some dirt with His saliva and rub it on a blind man's eyes was a symbol of health and life for first century Jews. As a result of this first century medicinal act, this blind man not only receives his sight, but symbolically represents both our faith life and our moral life.

For the second time in two weeks, the theme of our gospel readings draws us back to the subject of the healing waters of baptism, as represented by the waters of Siloam that the man is told to use for the cleansing of his eyes. What Jesus does today in the John is called by scripture scholars the sixth of the seven great miracles described in this particular gospel. Next week's miracle, the raising of Lazarus, symbolizes the eternal life awaiting those who choose to be washed clean and follow Christ. Essentially, what we are reading in today's gospel reminds us of the power of Christ's touch, Christ's presence and the water of baptism which reminds us of Christ's cleansing in our lives.

The beauty of this cleansing is that it does not stop at the sacrament of baptism. Every time we approach our Lord with a contrite heart, Jesus is willing and desiring to wash away our sins with the words of absolution offered in the confessional. Perhaps this is why the Holy Father challenged every diocese around the world to offer this sacrament in one of her parishes for twenty-four straight hours in what Pope Francis called, "A Feast of Forgiveness" that we will honor next Saturday, all day.

On this Laetare Sunday when we blend the darkness of purple with a touch of the Easter white, we come up with a rose color that allows us to look ahead just a little to recognize the full glory of Christ's presence that awaits us. Until that moment that we are removed from the shackles of the devil through God's intervention and our good lives, we resign ourselves to understand that the key to our salvation will *not* be endorsed neither by mothers nor doctors nor certainly our director of maintenance at St. Patrick's Church. The fact is, if you want to get to the kingdom of heaven... sometimes you have to play in the mud. This is our prayer.

5th Sunday of Lent (Ez 37: 12-14; Ps 130: 1-2, 3-4, 5-6, 7-8; Rm 8: 8-11; John 11: 1-45 or 11: 3-7, 17, 20-27, 33b-45)

During my life as a priest, I have crossed the path of the 11th Chapter of John on this 5th Sunday of Lent every single year. The assemblers of our Sunday Readings offer three cycles of readings which we are supposed to cover in sequence, but it dawned on me that every year that I have celebrated Mass on this particular Sunday, I have been honored to celebrate Mass in front of parishioners who were preparing to celebrate the Easter Sacraments in the upcoming days. Church rules instruct the priest to use the reading from the 11th Chapter of John when these faithful souls who wish to receive the Easter sacraments are present, so practically every year that I have celebrated Mass on this particular Sunday, I have preached on the raising of our dear brother Lazarus.

What has struck me is that during my life as a priest, I have focused on the exact same theme year after year, though the theme is not the prominent focus of today's gospel. Scripture scholars will tell us that the story of Jesus standing in front of Lazarus' tomb parallels the themes of death and resurrection that we commemorate during Holy Week.

However, the theme on which I have focused consistently in the Lazarus story rests on something that occurs very rarely in our gospel readings. The theme is this: *What does it take to make a savior cry?* Jesus doesn't cry much in the New Testament. Outside of weeping during His entry into Jerusalem in the 19th Chapter of Luke and His agony at Gethsemane, this passage may be the only other one I can think of where Jesus actually cries in the New Testament.

I think to myself that there are a lot of reasons why people cry in life. We often cry at both trivial and significant moments that we encounter, whether they be special awards, during the day of a wedding or anniversary or certainly at the passing of a loved one.

Scripture scholars differ as to the reason why Christ was so emotional in today's reading. Some claim that Jesus was *angry*, that Jesus was furious that the people that he taught and loved *just didn't get it*. As our Lord spent His time on earth teaching the ways of God to a people that followed Him, even after all His work, the people didn't get it. That same rule applies today. How many times have any of us disregarded the way of God in favor of our own values? How many times has God been furious at us for the way we turn away from the gospel in life?

The gospel reading depicts Jesus' emotion as that of being *disturbed,* an emotion connected to the type of sadness that Jesus encountered standing in front of the tomb of His friend. Imagine standing in a place where a loved one is resting, a place that reminds you of the emptiness that exists with your loved one's departure, an emptiness that recalls our own human condition and the shortness of life that we experience on earth. Imagine that you knew your immediate future, that you knew about the sufferings and type of death that you were about to encounter, which becomes all too real when reflecting about life and death issues on earth. For me, I often turn to the Lamentation Psalms during this time of grief, especially the ones from Psalm 51 and Psalm 22: "My God, my God, why have you abandoned me?" "Have mercy on me, O God, in your goodness, in your abundant compassion wipe out my offense. Wash away all my guilt and cleanse me of my sin."

Our gospel reading illustrates today many of the great symbols that we will encounter on His way to the Good Friday celebration and the Passion of our Lord. We will read about Jesus' suffering and death, the resting in the tomb, the wailing of the faithful and ultimately the resurrection. As we reflect on those symbols and begin to pray the psalms and the words of faith, I think all of us can understand in this light why Jesus would cry at this moment in His ministry. If any of us were to know the means by which you were to end your life on earth, then I think any of us would reflect the same type of emotions that our Lord did at that moment.

Whenever I get to those moments of grief, I turn to the end of those psalms of Lament and I look to the end of the psalms, which remind me that the sufferings of the present will always be replaced with the joy and the grace of our Lord that is yet to come on the other side of the precipice that separates the heavens from the earth. "Rescue me from my death, O Lord, for when you open my lips, my mouth shall declare your praise. For my sacrifice, O Lord, is a broken heart and a humble, contrite heart you will not spurn." Even today's psalm of Lament from chapter 130 ends with a plea of Love to our Lord: "For with the LORD is kindness, with Him is full redemption and God will redeem Israel from all their sins."

The most comforting prayer I have been utilizing as of late comes from the 16th Chapter of John's gospel, a text we often use at funeral liturgies of our faithful, where our Lord offers solace to His apostles who prepare themselves to be parted from the Lord themselves. In His words of consolation, the Lord speaks,

> "Do not let your hearts be troubled. You have faith in God; have faith also in me. In my Father's house there are many dwelling places. If there were not, would I have told you that I am going to prepare a place for you? If I go and prepare a place for you, I will come back again and take you to myself, so that where I am you also may be. Where I am going you know the way." Thomas said to Him, "Master, we do not know where you are going; how can we

know the way?"

Jesus said to him, "I am the way and the truth and the life. No one comes to the Father except through me."[xiii]

It seems to me that the only way to reach the joy of Easter is to cry during Lent, to be mad enough, sad enough to do something about the injustices in the world. It is important that we become moved by the example of others in this community, moved enough that we follow that example and become the example for others. It seems to me that the tears God sheds for those who follow His path are those of joy and love rather than loathe and sorrow. But it requires a response from the faithful. It requires us to carry the cross and sacrifice ourselves to others so that we show God the degree by which we wish to follow Him.

So let us have a good cry today. Let us be sad and mad at the injustices of the world. If we can feel the lack of love in the world, then we will be compelled to do something about it. For when we realize the depths of sadness that our Lord was willing to endure for us, then we realize our Lord is willing to carry us beyond the precipice to an existence where there will be no more tears, no more suffering and no more death. Let us allow the Lord to carry us through this void of death and guide others to follow this path as well. This is our prayer.

Palm Sunday [Mt 21: 1-11 (procession); Is 50: 4-7; Ps 22: 8-9, 17-18, 19-20, 23-24; Phil 2: 6-11; Mt 26: 14 – 27: 66 or 27: 11-54]

Have you ever seen the cartoon where a tiny snowball rolls down a mountain, collects vast amounts of white goodness as it builds up momentum and eventually becomes this monster-sized snowball that runs over anything in its path? Kids get a kick out of watching these goofy images portrayed in a cartoon, but many times we have real-life experiences like this which aren't funny at all. Whenever we see the way that a hurricane grows over the body of an ocean, or how a brush fire builds up fierce enough to destroy a forest, or even how one person's sin can spread and affect all the people around them, we often grimace at the power of such disastrous situations

As I was reading the Passion reading from Matthew, I was thinking how one person's sin escalated into a full-blown mob scene, resulting in our Lord's death. First, Judas Iscariot betrays Jesus. Judas' sin was the match that lit the fire of the Sanhedrin. Peter was not strong enough to put out the fire – he actually avoided the devastation by denying his Lord three times. The disciples did not confront the storm; instead, they went into hiding. Even the once faithful people that greeted the Lord on His final entrance into Jerusalem eventually turned on Him, good people who joined in the riots that the Sanhedrin started and sentenced to death the one person who could give us hope. We commemorate Palm Sunday by realizing that very few people defended the Lord then, begging the

Rev. Peter G. Jankowski

question as to how many of us would defend the Lord in today's age, if we were located in the same predicament.

If there is one last lesson to learn during the Season of Lent, it is this: one sin can affect many people. In order to move into Easter, we must learn that sin is contagious and the only cure for it is by living a Christ-centered life, a life full of God's love. Over the last 2000 years, we have experienced many mob scenes that have escalated from one person's anger, whether it be that of the Neros, Napoleons or Hitlers of the later ages. Even today in our world, we have outbreaks of violence that build to full-scale wars, whether it be in the Middle East, the Koreas, in the countries surrounding Russia and even on the streets of America. Who is strong enough to stand up to this oppression?

But in this country, we do not experience the pains of war like other countries do. We are much better off financially and otherwise. What disheartens me is that the momentum against the faith is not through violence, but through ambivalence. When one person shows how little they care about their faith, then this experience affects those around them and if we are not careful this lack of care spreads and builds up momentum within itself.

The only way to combat the violence and ambivalence of the world is through building a momentum of love, by coming together in this Church and making a difference in the things that we do. Christ dying on that cross for our salvation was the greatest act of love we could ever experience. We remember what Christ did because His love has been growing for 2000 years and we experience that love every time we gather together and share the faith with each other.

Over the next few days, we all will have an opportunity to share this faith in the various sacred services that take place in this very Holy Week. On Thursday, Friday and Saturday nights, we celebrate the three most intense, love-filled liturgies that we have in the entire year. If we really want to show God and each other how this momentum is growing in our lives, then we make a difference by first sharing in Christ's suffering and great love on our behalf.

May we be able to build up the momentum of God's love as we approach Easter by reconciling with those who we treated badly. Let us come together and love together so that we may see Easter together. This is our prayer.

Holy Thursday (Ex 12: 1-8, 11-14; Ps 116: 12-13, 15-16, 17-18; 1 Cor 11: 23-26; John 13: 1-15)

"This homily is presented to you through the generosity of the United States Post Office"

Earlier today, I took my turn celebrating Mass over at the Stateville Correctional facility in Crest Hill, Illinois. As I really am not supposed to celebrate two Masses on Holy Thursday, I was put in a quandary. I am also not the pope – if I tried to celebrate Mass at the prison and had someone else celebrate Mass at my parish on Holy Thursday like he did at St. Peter's Basilica, I don't think my bishop would have been too thrilled. So I decided to offer the inmates a scripture service with the traditional foot washing ceremony on Thursday morning. By doing so, I could still channel the spirit of Pope Francis in my actions without celebrating two Masses on this most sacred day.

So I arrived at the prison on Thursday morning, realizing that I would have to make do with whatever resources I could find at Stateville, since I would not be permitted to bring anything into the prison without a pre-approved gate pass. The prison would not have a flagon available for me to pour water so we found a yellowing milk carton into which we poured the fresh, clean, brown Crest Hill water that we would use for foot washing. Cloth towels were certainly not available to us so we ended up using paper towels from the kitchen. As we had no chance of finding respectable bowls into which we could place under the feet of the inmates who came forward, all we had available to us was the same type of plastic United States mail tub that I show you today.

In the end, with that brown water from the yellow jug with the paper towels and the plastic mail tub, I was able to wash the feet of the nine prisoners who volunteered to have their feet washed on Holy Thursday morning. I tried to cajole three others into participating in the rite but I think the rest of the inmates were afraid of the mail tub.

From this experience, I came to find my inspiration for today's homily. As I was washing the feet of those who came forward this morning, I began to reflect on the life of the postal worker whose work ethic, according to their motto, states that "Neither snow nor rain nor heat nor gloom of night stays these couriers from the swift completion of their appointed rounds." I began to reflect on our own local postal carrier, a nice enough woman of middle age, who dutifully comes to our rectory each day to share a few kind words while exchanging the incoming mail with the outgoing mail. Every so often, our rectory's sixty-pound noise maker, Rusty Joe the basset hound, makes an appearance during our postal lady's rounds, giving her his sniff of approval before she heads out the door. As is Rusty's tradition, as soon as the nice postal worker leaves the house, Rusty jumps up and down from where he stands, spins around a few times and barks vociferously as to say, "How come I don't get to go outside, too?"

I can only imagine how this poor woman has to walk the streets every day, encountering the various creatures on two and four legs that she does while dutifully bringing all of us our daily correspondences. I can only imagine how some folks that she encounters are friendly enough and how some others are probably less than friendly. Lord only knows how often she has to dodge the dogs and cats and other beasts of the day that cross her path. Concerning her job, I keep thinking about how thankless her job probably is and how the only responses that ever gets reported about her conduct, good or bad, come from those who do not get their mail on any certain day.

So goes the life of ministry. To become evangelists like Christ, to spread the gospel message throughout the world, we encounter those who are receptive to the message and we encounter many others who are not so receptive, knowing that more often than not the only response often reported are those times when something goes wrong rather than when something is done right.

Which brings me back to the prison... As I washed the feet of these nine men, I couldn't help but think about this example of service that Jesus offered on the night before died, according to John's gospel. This morning, I started reflecting on Jesus' suffering and death, thinking about how many of the apostles at the time of His death actually defended the life of our Lord at the most critical of times. In the gospel of Matthew, none of the apostles were found at the foot of the cross. In the gospel of Mark, you will find none of the apostles as well. The same can be said in the gospel of Luke and in John's gospel, only one of the apostles was present at the crucifixion, most likely alluding to the apostle for whom the gospel was named (showing favoritism to the head of the Johannine community). We certainly know that one of the apostles purposely handed His teacher to the members of the Sanhedrin (Matthew tells us the price for Jesus' head was thirty pieces of silver) and another denied that he knew the Lord on three occasions that fateful night.

Out of forty-eight opportunities to support our Lord during His Passion and Death within the four gospel stories (Twelve Apostles times four gospels), our Lord was only supported *once* (by "the apostle whom Jesus loved" in John's gospel) *and* yet our Lord still chose to wash the feet of His apostles anyway! You could say that a postal worker delivers mail because it's their job but you can tell the difference between a person going through the motions and a person who loves what they do. Many times, you can tell the same about a cleric or even a person who chooses to attach the title "Christian" to their name. The answer is a simple one – you serve others, even those who abandon you, because you choose not to abandon them because you still have hope in them.

The story of Christ washing the apostles' feet in John's gospel is supposed to be a model for all of us evangelizing the people of the world, starting in our own community. Take a look around you, whether it be in our church, our neighborhood or even our world. If you cannot, or do not wish to, wash the feet of the people next to you or allow them to do the same for us, even if they do not accept you or love you, then we are not ready to enter the kingdom of heaven. Conversely, if we follow Christ's path and make every effort to wash someone else's feet, especially those who are the poorest and most downtrodden, then we truly understand the meaning of Christian service and this example of service that I am about to offer in Christ's name might have meaning for those who are truly committed to serve.

For this reason, I felt compelled to honor my promise to serve those in the prison this morning. I realize that my presence to some in the prison is *not* welcome, but like life, this is the response to ministry as well. Unless I can live out fully the challenge set by St. Paul the apostle in the eighth chapter of Romans or even the credo of the US Post Office in a Christian context, then the action I am about to do will have no meaning for me as well. St. Paul states, "Neither height nor depth nor angels nor principalities nor powers will ever separate us from the love of God through His son our Lord Jesus Christ" (paraphrase of Romans 8: 35-39); my version of the Post Office credo states that "Neither snow nor rain nor heat nor gloom of night stays these ministers from the swift completion of Christian service." Unless I live this, I will find it difficult to reach my destination in heaven. As hard as I find this ministry to be as a priest and as a Christian, it pales to the infinitely more difficult sacrifice that we commemorate at tomorrow's Good Friday service.

May we learn how to wash the feet of others by service others, *all others,* in the name of Christ. This is how we give honor to what we are about to do. This is our prayer today.

Good Friday (Is 52: 13 - 53: 12; Ps 31: 2-6, 12-13, 15-16, 17-25; Heb 4: 14-16; 5: 7-9; John 18: 1 - 19: 42)

Welcome to the 14th Day of Nisan.

For us simple folks here living here on Marion & Willow, the particular nuance of this date may not mean much to us. In fact, many in these pews might be just as satisfied to be told that today is simply "Good Friday," the day we commemorate the death of the Lord. If I may be so bold, I would like to add one layer to our commemoration of this day, because the focus on which John's gospel places the importance of this day is a focus that symbolizes this event way too dramatically to overlook.

In this light, I want to mention how the author of John's gospel makes a slight change from Matthew, Mark and Luke in the timeline of Jesus' death. In reality, John's Gospel places Jesus' death not on the day *after* Passover but rather *one day earlier,* the

14th Day of Nisan, on the morning *before* the Passover meal. If we understand the chronology of John's gospel to be true, then Jesus' Last Supper was not a Passover at all and we lose a bit of continuity between the four gospel narratives.

Why would St. John make such a change? Why is this narrative fluctuation so important?

For St. John, the change is important due the significance he places on the symbolism of the *lambs* of the Passover rather than the Passover meal itself. In the first century, the Jewish faithful believed that during the Passover celebrations, they were forbidden to offer any sacrifices of lambs or any other animals, since the time the spent with their family and with their God was extremely sacred. According to their custom, the Jewish faithful would sacrifice these young lambs to remind themselves that on in the 12th Chapter of the Book of Exodus, the era of Father Moses, the faithful were instructed to smear the blood of these baby lambs on the lintels of their houses as a sign for the Lord to "pass over" their houses so that their children would be spared.

In this symbolism, the Jewish faithful since that time were instructed to offer this same type of sacrifice as an offering to the Lord for the sake of his protection and love.

St. John changed the meaning of this symbol in the suffering and death of Jesus Christ.

According to St. John's Gospel chronology, at the same time that Jesus died on the afternoon of this 14th Day of Nisan, many of the Jewish faithful were preparing for the Passover Meal by sacrificing these baby lambs within the walls of Jerusalem. St. John called the 14th of Nisan "The Day of Preparation" prior to the Passover, a preparation that became quite ironic in the world of faith, since the Messiah that the faithful sought to encounter at that meal was the same person that was hung on the cross. According to the symbolism of the gospel story we have just heard, no other lambs would ever need to be sacrificed, for the last, final and infinitely most important sacrifice has been offered for us by this new Lamb of God, who takes away the sins of all salvation through this one act.

Whereas before this act the fate of a sinful human race was in question, after this act the salvation for those who imitate the Lamb of God through their own sacrifice and love becomes plainly evident. As stated in a homily from St. Melito of Sardis, one of our great saints from the late second century:

> The law is old, but the gospel is new; the type was for a time, but grace is forever. The sheep was corruptible, but the Lord is incorruptible, who was crushed as a lamb, but who was resurrected as God. For although was led to sacrifice as a sheep, yet was not a sheep; and although was as a lamb without voice, yet indeed was not a lamb. The one was the model; the other was found to be the finished product. For God replaced the lamb and a man the sheep; but in the man was Christ, who contains all things.[xiv]

In yesterday's homily, I spoke about the importance of this word "sacrifice," a word which defines the word "Mass" and the type of lifestyle that we are all called to lead. In today's liturgy, we are shown the infinitely most graphic of ways what kind of suffering needs to be evident in order to be called truly, "the lamb of God." Since our Lord's death, one martyr after another have suffered the pains of execution in one horrific way after another. These individual sufferings took place for the sake of Christ; the sufferings of Christ took place for the sake of salvation. When we live like the lambs and shepherds of today's age, we provide the opportunity to open the eyes of others who might not otherwise have been able to recognize what the sufferings of the Lamb of God was truly about.

In some ways, this 14th Day of Nisan proves to be a fulcrum for the entire Triduum experience within the faith life of our Church today. Our Catechism teaches us that our Easter celebration usually falls on the Sunday after the first full moon after the first day of spring and in early times full moon took place on the 14th Day of Nisan.

As a resurrection people within this country, we often look forward to the Easter story by glancing over the story of Christ's Passion. However, the faithful Catholic surely understands the import of what our Lord has done for us on this particular day, in an era when sin and desolation and the work of Satan appears to be just as strong as it was some 2000 years ago. For the faithful Catholic, we realize that we *need* to embrace this lamb of God who is willing to bear our sins, suffer for us today and offer us hope in today's age, as well as in any age. As St. Melito of Sardis assures us,

> Therefore, come, all families of men, you who have been befouled with sins and receive forgiveness for your sins. I am your forgiveness, I am the Passover

of your salvation, I am the lamb which was sacrificed for you, I am your ransom, I am your light, I am your savior, I am your resurrection, I am your king, I am leading you up to the heights of heaven, I will show you the eternal Father, I will raise you up by my right hand.

This is the alpha and the omega. This is the beginning and the end – an indescribable beginning and an incomprehensible end. This is the Christ. This is the king. This is Jesus. This is the general. This is the Lord. This is the one who rose up from the dead. This is the one who sits at the right hand of the Father. bears the Father and is borne by the Father, to whom be the glory and the power forever.[xv]

Let us realize that the story we read today, albeit tragic and horrific, is a story of hope, according to John's Gospel, which assures us that the stain of this death of faith will never touch the hearts of those who believe.

Lamb of God, you take away the sins of the world. Have mercy on us.
Lamb of God, you take away the sins of the world. Have mercy on us.
Lamb of God, you take away the sins of the world. Grant us peace.

Let us pray.

Father, look with love upon your people, the love which our Lord Jesus Christ showed us when delivered Himself to evil men and suffered the agony of the cross, for lives and reigns with you and the Holy Spirit, one God, forever and ever. Amen.[xvi]

This is our prayer.

Stories on the Journey: The Season of Easter (Cycle A Homilies)

The Solemnity of Easter

The Bundle of Sticks (An Aesop Fable)

An old man on the point of death summoned his sons around him to give them some parting advice. ordered his servants to bring in a bundle of sticks and said to his eldest son: "Break it." The son strained and strained, but with all his efforts was unable to break the bundle. The other sons also tried, but none of them was successful. "Untie the bundle," said the father, "and each of you take a stick." When they had done so, he called out to them: "Now, break the stick," and each stick was easily broken. "You see my meaning," said their father.[xvii]

Do you all understand the moral of this story? Do you understand how this story fits into the context of the Catholic Church? If we untie this bundle of sticks, possible the moral will become more evident.

This stick represents the English speaking community.

This stick represents the Spanish speaking community.

This stick represents the black community.

Rev. Peter G. Jankowski

This stick represents the Asian and Filipino community.

This stick represents those in our parish who are poor and in need of financial hope.

This stick represents those who are homeless and without any shelter.

This stick represents those who are hungry and without any food.

This stick represents those who are elderly and unable to come to Mass on Sundays.

This stick represents those who are suffering because of mental, emotional or financial difficulties.

To be honest, we could be assigning sticks to every group that makes up part of the Church, from the poor to the rich to those of different languages, customs and ways of life. Separately, each of these sticks can easily be broken; we can easily eradicate any number of groups in our parish through violence, acts of loathe or even bad thoughts or words. As this building has existed almost one hundred years, one simple act or insurgency could destroy this building as easily as it was created.

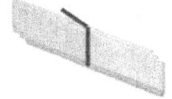 Or we can bundle the sticks together and allow God to establish a Church that is indestructible.

We have learned during the Season of Lent that our lives are fragile and our lives are sinful. Without God's help, we often succumb to sin because we are vulnerable people who easily can be manipulated and broken. We have learned that without Christ's help, we would be lost and without hope. We have learned that the Word of God came into our existence to carry the burden of our sins on that cross so that we might have another chance to right ourselves with God.

Here is the beauty of the faith – if we accept this mission of Christ by not just learning it but *living it,* then we realize that the joy of the Christian faith is to assemble the lost and vulnerable and give them the hope they so desperately seek. This is the theme that St. Paul offers in his First Letter to the Corinthians – it is up to the strong in the faith to carry those who are week by loving them, serving them, feeding them and protecting them. As St. Francis teaches us, it is in giving that we receive, in pardoning that we are pardoned and it is in dying that we are born to eternal life.

Prior to Lent or Advent, the leadership in most Catholic Churches take time to visit one particular, vulnerable and sacred group within the parish community, namely our homebound brothers and sisters who cannot be with us at the Masses this weekend. I benefit greatly from these visits because those we visit are so grateful for what we offer them and both of us are the recipients of their loving gratitude.

However, by no stretch of the imagination do I believe that the presence of the Holy Spirit is made possibly solely by my work alone. In order for these visits to take place, our parish's Office Manager calls each of our homebound to set up appointments for us to come and visit those who are in need. Our Director of Religious Education takes the time to braid crosses from last week's palms for those homebound in our community. The children from our Religious Education Program devote time in the classroom to make cards for our homebound by their own hands. Because of your generosity, we gift each homebound brother or sister with Easter lily plants in the spring and Poinsettia plants in the winter. For us to visit the homebound at St. Patrick's, first we need to seek out the core members of our parish to help us with this most important ministry.

Is not the work of the evangelist? Is this not what our baptismal calling is all about? As Jesus was baptized, so are we; as Jesus ministered to those who are poor in spirit, so we follow that example. As Jesus calls us to be evangelists for the next generation, so we follow that call by living like Christ and imitating His example.

Whether it be a grandparent, an uncle, a fiancée, a DRE, a Parish Office Manager, deacons, priests, bishops or all the lay folks here in this community, every person in this worship space, tall or small, old or young, has the great capacity to serve as an evangelist in our Church, an evangelization which always starts in the home and moves its way outward. When we pray at home, serve at home and study at home, we set the example of how we should live and this example builds the kingdom of God one stick at a time.

Then when we carry that message outside of the home, when we invite our neighbors and our friends to join us in prayer, we end up with such an overflowing crowd because of this invitation to what I call "the empty cave," to invite those to meet the presence of Christ in the word, the Eucharist, through the priest *In Persona Christi* and certainly through the presence of God that lives within you.

For the last year and a half, our Holy Father Francis has been repeating this theme on a constant basis that our responsibility in the faith must begin with the role of the evangelist, both in church, at home and in this community. At a talk this January when he spoke about our response to the baptismal calling, Pope Francis said the following:

> In virtue of Baptism we become *missionary disciples*, called to bring the Gospel to the world (cf. Apostolic Exhortation *Evangelii Gaudium*, n. 120). "All the baptized, whatever their position in the Church or their level of instruction in the faith, are agents of evangelization.... The new evangelization calls for personal involvement" (*ibid.*) from everyone, the whole of the People of God, a new kind of personal involvement on the part of each of the baptized. The People of God is *a disciple People* — because it receives the faith — and *a missionary People* — because it transmits the faith. This is what Baptism works in us: it gives us Grace and hands on the faith to us. All of us in the Church are disciples and this we are forever,

our whole lifelong; and we are all missionaries, each in the place the Lord has assigned to him or her. Everyone: the littlest one is also a missionary; and the one who seems to be the greatest is a disciple. But one of you might say: "Bishops are not disciples, Bishops know everything; the Pope knows everything, he is not a disciple". No, the Bishops and the Pope must also be disciples, because if they are not disciples, they do no good. They cannot be missionaries; they cannot transmit the faith. We must all be disciples and missionaries.[xviii]

My hope and prayer this Easter Season is that those in this community might take the Holy Father's words to heart and live out that life of evangelization in our parish community so that the lessons of Lent and Easter may be made manifest by our thoughts and example.

You are all sacred and special. You all represent a most important part of this parish. Like the sticks that make up a bundle, we wish to strengthen you by loving you; all we ask is that you do the same for each other, as we build this faith life of St. Patrick's... *one stick at a time.*

May you all have a Blessed and Holy Easter Season! This is our prayer.

2nd Sunday of Easter (Acts 2: 42-47; Ps 118: 2-4, 13-15, 22-24; 1 Pet 1: 3-9; John 20: 19-31)

> I would not, could not, in a box
> I would not, could not, with a fox.
> I will not eat them in a house
> I will not eat them with a mouse.
> I will not eat them here or there,
> I will not eat them anywhere.
> I will not eat Green Eggs and Ham,
> I will not eat them, Sam I Am![xix]

The Dr. Seuss story of <u>Green Eggs and Ham</u> is one of those classics that every child should know and read, because the basic values taught in that book transcend different generations. Let's face it – at one time or another, all of us have questions or doubts about the realities of society, whether it be something economic, social, or spiritual. We are told information that we sometimes <u>have</u> to question, information about the economy or the way we raise our children to name a couple. If we have doubts, we ultimately don't believe. We're like that guy in the story who won't try or accept something because he or she doesn't understand.

The key to the Seuss book, our lives, the key to the gospel, is *trust*. Do we trust someone else enough that we can place our lives in their hands and take a chance? Risk is such a daunting thing in our lives and it has a great potential of damage, but it also has a great potential for joy. Take, for instance, a dating relationship. If you ever want to find that special person in your life, you have to take that risk. You have to expose yourself to another person and trust that person enough to accept you for who you are. As we know in life, there are some relationships where the trust factor pays off and some relationships where it doesn't.

Then there's Christ. Here's a God that comes down on earth with no other motive than to love. He floods us with love by healing us, saving us, dying and rising for us and giving us this meal so that we can be nourished. All asks of us is to trust Him enough to follow His example of loving God and loving our neighbor. But like the guy in Dr. Seuss, we are hesitant; we do not want to trust, because caution is the way of the human being. I cannot imagine any of us giving into anything without condition, but that is what God exactly is asking us to do.

If we trust, if we take that chance and give in to the Lord, what we get back is phenomenal. Unfortunately, we act like Thomas – we ask for proof or some tangent sign that God exists before we give into Him. We want to see the hands and the feet; we want to see the nail marks before we take that chance with Christ.

It seems that doubt proves to be our downfall. Ultimately, if we depend on some kind of scientific fact to prove or understand God, then we will fail, because our God is not found in science but in our hearts and souls. The seed of God cannot be proven but lived and most of all found in prayer. In all the books that Thomas Aquinas wrote about God, ultimately writes that the truth about God he does not know; none of us do. The call to knowing God is the call to faith and that requires us to take a leap into something that ultimately we cannot comprehend.

So my prayer for you (and for all of us) is that we turn away from the doubts of faith and turn to Christ's love. May we always share the prayer of Dr. Seuss with the people of the world, a faith that proclaims...

> I want to share it in a box
> I want to share it with a fox.
> I shall now, shall now in a house
> I shall now, shall now with a mouse.
> I want to spread love here and there,
> I want to spread love everywhere
> I love to share faith when I can,
> Thank you, thank you, Sam I Am!

Thank you, God, for your gift of love! This is our prayer.

3rd Sunday of Easter (Acts 2: 14, 22-33; Ps 16: 1-2a-5, 7-8, 9-10, 11; 1 Pet 1: 17-21; Luke 24: 13-35)

Every so often, I like to take the time for a walk around the city of Joliet. When I was weight-conscious fifteen years ago, my journey would consist of five parishes – St. Paul's, St. Ray's, St. Mary Nativity, a stop at the chancery for a piece of candy and a word with the secretary, St. Mary Nativity, St. Pat's and to St. Paul's. Now that I am weight-conscious"less," my trip pretty much takes me from St. Pat's to McDonald's and back with the basset dog in hand.

During this two-mile quest that satisfies me with a Diet Coke and the dog with a plain double cheeseburger, I noticed that my basset hound has pretty much conditioned me to do his bidding during our time together. On the way to McDonalds, the ritual for my dog Rusty-Joe remains the same – *Pull, Sniff and Pour*. On the way to McDonald's, Rusty tends to pull me and drag me to whatever tree or fire hydrant he can find so that he can perform the traditional dog ritual.

On the way back from McDonalds, the ritual for Rusty-Joe is a little different – *Pull, Sniff and Plop*. For the return, I usually am the one that has to drag Rusty and he will find any excuse he can to sniff the flowers and lay down on a cold surface. Needless to say, the trip back to the parish is usually the slower and more difficult part of the walk.

Actually, what makes the walks worthwhile is that every so often, I pass by someone I know from the parish or I see people at work in their daily lives. I see the parent mowing the lawn or the kids playing in the street. I see the lovers making "googlie-eyes" at each other or college students studying intensely on their way to school. I also have noticed that, now that I have the dog in tow, I often do not nor cannot pay attention to the world that surrounds me because a four-legged hound seems to want to attract all of my interest.

In reflection of my walks with Rusty and the theme for today's gospel, I think how I often take the people I pass down the street for granted, passing them by while preoccupied with the diva of a quadruped that tugs me down the street. I also notice that when I take the same walks alone, my pace during the journey is not as quick and I can devote more time for the important things that pass me by. Without

Rusty, my attention is not diverted so I can focus more clearly on my surroundings, observing the people who go about their daily business. On these occasions of clarity, I feel almost, no <u>exactly</u> like I can see the face of God passing by in the hearts of people that I meet.

Maybe my faith life at times has a sense of a "mom shut off switch" in reverse. For me when I am with Rusty, I often notice that nothing else is more important than caring for his needs, which a mom constantly does in her life. However, moms have a specific gift that I wish I could possess at times – moms have the innate ability, even with all the kids wreaking havoc in the home, of tuning them out in order to focus on whatever task is at hand for them.

At times, I wish I could tune out better, especially during times of prayer. At times, I wish I could tune in better to God's word as well.

Don't we all have the problem in the world of faith? How many times does God try to speak to us in our daily lives, only to have us "tune him out" in favor of whatever thought, task or leisurely activity we have at hand? How many times when God is trying to talk to me do I not tune the world out, enabling me to focus myself in such a way that I can better listen to what he has to say? How often am I negligent in my daily prayers, in my silence, in my adoration and even when listening to the readings at Mass?

As I was taking a walk with the pooch this week, I was thinking about the fact that Christ has been walking with me down this path all my life. He has been talking to me and has been revealing Himself to me in the face of every person that comes my way. In essence, the Lord has been within me and all around me at every moment of my life. At times, I cannot help but wonder if my entire life is an Emmaus moment and whether I can recognize the Lord outside of the breaking of the bread.

As we walk on this road, Christ walks with us, behind us and all around us. As I reflected on my walk this week, as I couldn't help but think of the prayer of St. Patrick of Ireland lived out in the flesh through those called to present us the face of Christ all around us, behind us, above us and within us. Through their charity, through your charity, the Emmaus Story at St. Patrick's tells us how Christ walks with us on this journey and shares every experience with us in this world every moment of our lives.

Let us be challenged today to open our eyes and ears to the love of Christ in the world. As our prayer today, let us listen to those words attributed to St. Patrick of Ireland, words that call us to the face of God which walks with us on our journey through life, a prayer with which I would like to end my homily:

> Christ with me, Christ before me,
>   Christ behind me,
> Christ in me, Christ beneath me, Christ above me,
> Christ on my right hand, Christ on my left,
> Christ where I lie, Christ where I sit,
> Christ where I arise,
>
> Christ in the heart of everyone who thinks of me,
> Christ in the mouth of everyone who speaks to me,
> Christ in every eye that sees me,
> Christ in every ear that hears me.
> Salvation is of the Lord; Salvation is of Christ.

May your salvation, O Lord, Be ever with us. Amen.[xx]

This is our prayer.

4th Sunday of Easter (Acts 2: 14a, 36-41; Ps 23: 1-3a, 3b-4, 5, 6; 1 Pet 2: 20b-25; John 10: 1-10)

During my last summer before I was ordained a priest, I took part in a Hospital ministry program called "Clinical Pastoral Education" or CPE. My seminary required all students to take a summer of CPE so that we had some experience in grief ministry prior to our ordinations.

Now for me, I have often preached about CPE being one of the most difficult yet rewarding ministries in which I have been involved. As a priest, grief ministry can be the most appreciative form of service when you invest yourself in the lives of people who are suffering and it also can be the worst ministry when you do not make time for these same people. I have found that outside of the sacraments, caring for the sick and dying is one of the most important things I do as a priest.

During my ten-week encounter in CPE, I was assigned to Edward Hospital in Naperville, Illinois. I loved Edward Hospital. The head chaplain there was an American Baptist by faith, extremely open and understanding to the people of all faith traditions who worked with her. The floor I was assigned was the Cardio Vascular Care Unit (or CVCU). I loved the CVCU, or the "heart floor," as I called it. As a general rule, anyone who had a successful heart operation received a second lease on life and entering the room of a heart patient became very heartening to a future priest who searched for hope during difficult times.

On the other hand, I also had opportunities to visit patients on the Oncology, or Cancer Ward, as well. I often found the Cancer Ward to be much more difficult than the Heart Floor, since many patients who were treated for cancer often had to face the inevitable conclusion of life's all too short brevity on earth. It was on the Oncology Floor that an experience took place for me that became the inspiration for today's homily.

During my time at Edward Hospital, I carried a beeper twice a week and served as the emergency chaplain for those who were in grief. One night, I received a page from the Oncology Floor. I was told that an elderly woman was dying from cancer and that her husband asked for their local parish priest to be with them during these last moments of life. I called the parish priest in Naperville, but he told me that he would need a half an hour before he could arrive at the hospital.

Now here I am, a young, naïve recruit who had limited experience in hospital ministry, trying to bide a half an hour's time with this grieving husband. I was new to hospital ministry – this was my first experience with this type of suffering. As I entered the room, this man was on his knees at his wife's bedside, crying to God and asking our Lord what to do. The man was obviously lost in his predicament. I sat down and tried not to disturb the man, yet wanting to do something that would be of help.

After a couple of minutes of soul-searching, I recalled the one psalm that I learned by heart in the seminary, my old "stand-by" prayer that serves me well to this day when I am at a loss for words. I began to recite Psalm 23, the psalm for our Mass today and began to pray this psalm over and over and over again. I kept praying the following:

The Lord is my shepherd; I shall not want
In verdant pastures gives me repose
Besides restful waters leads me; refreshes my soul.
He guides me on right paths for His name's sake.
And though I walk in the dark valley, I fear no evil
For you are at my side,
with your rod and your staff to give me courage.
You spread the table before me in the sight of my foes.
You anoint my head with oil; my cup overflows.
Only goodness and kindness shall follow me all the days of my life
I shall dwell in the house of the Lord for years to come.[xxi]

After about 10-15 minutes of this recitation, I finally remained silent, not knowing what to do or say. As I sat there and watched this man suffer, I quietly asked God to offer this man comfort and peace during this difficult time.

A short time later, the man's wife passed away.

It was the moment right after the woman died that the pastor of this man's church walked into the room. Now the best way I can describe this man was that of a grandfather, the kind of nice, old guy whom a lot of people might overlook in the corner of the room but serves as the leaning post for those who need to talk and the wise sage to whom others turn for advice.

As "Fr. Grandpa" walked into the room, the disposition of the grieving man immediately began to change. I don't think that the priest spoke more than five words in the entire conversation (something like, "How are you doing, Bill?"), but as soon as he arrived, the husband began to talk about his wife. Bill talked about his 50+ years of marriage, his kids and grandkids, the love he had for his spouse and how deeply he will miss her. The kindly priest escorted Bill into one of the nearby waiting rooms, allowing him to speak to his heart's content. When Bill had finished telling his story one half hour later, the priest volunteered to drive him home that night. "Don't worry about your car," the priest assured him, "your children can pick it up tomorrow morning." With those words, Bill and his parish priest left the hospital, never to be seen by me again.

If I ever wanted to know what a sheep gate looked like, that parish priest served that role to a tee. For those of faith, the gate that opens one's life to the sacred is easily accessible and wonderful to experience. To those who choose not to experience this gate, it is those who try to experience the divine like a thief, for they have no idea how to experience God through building a simple relationship. It was because of a presence of God found within the window of this priest that the husband could find compassion from the divine, the same kind of compassion that is found in the hearts of anyone who extends their lives to those in need of love and support.

As we reach the halfway point of the Easter Season, may all of us realize that we serve as the gate to the divine as well. Our actions and words are able to serve as the entry way to God, if we allow God to flow through us. The same example of this priest's love can be found in our love as well. May we embrace this love, recognize God's presence within it and share it with the people that we meet. This is our prayer.

5th Sunday of Easter (Acts 6: 1-7; Ps 33: 1-2, 4-5, 18-19; 1 Pet 2: 4-9; John 14: 1-12)

Over the last few weeks, I have been spending a great deal of time instructing our children about the visible differences that distinguish a deacon, priest and bishop during liturgical celebrations in church. The differences begin with the use of a *stole,* a long strip of cloth that is worn over one shoulder to signify the office of the deacon and over both shoulders to signify the priest. I explained to the students that one main difference between a priest and a deacon is that a deacon can officiate at two of the seven sacraments (baptism and marriage) while a priest can officiate at six of the seven (the exception being Holy Orders, ordaining another priest or deacon).

When a priest is holding a shepherd's staff or *crosier,* places a miter over his head and wears a zucchetto (or a "beanie") underneath the miter, that person is designated as the head priest, or *bishop,* of the diocese. If the beanie is purple, then the bishop heads a diocese or assists another bishop. If the beanie is red, then the bishop is assigned to be a cardinal, who is installed to elect another pope. If the beanie is white, then the bishop is the pope, the most important bishop within the Catholic Church.

In addition to the other accoutrements that a priest wears, covering all of them is what is called a *chasuble,* or the outer garment that signifies royalty with God. I have been teaching kids that the Latin word for chasuble, *casula,* literally means "little house," the place under which the presence of God rests. This theme parallels today's gospel, where Christ tells His disciples that God has many houses of dwelling, symbolized by each and every one of us. Every time we receive the body of Christ, we *become* that house inside which the sacred presence of God dwells. Pope Benedict once wrote that the hands that hold this Precious Body actually become a tabernacle or table that receives a gift that is brought into our house. This chasuble symbolizes the role that each one of us serves as a vessel of Christ within the world.

It is the first reading, though, that is the focus of my homily, a reading that is highlighted by a liturgical garment called a *dalmatic,* the garment that a deacon wears during liturgical celebrations. In the first reading, seven men were chosen from the community of believers to preach the word of God and to assist the apostles in their mission. Primary among the deacons was St. Stephen, who holds the honor of representing the first martyr of the Church following our Lord's own death and whose feast day we celebrate on December 26th. It was Stephen who was called to serve and yet his service was a very difficult one, one that required him to sacrifice his life in defense of the faith.

Why would St. Stephen endure such hardship for the sake of faith? I think that the reason underlies the ministry of deacon, a word that, from the Greek word *diakonia*, is translated as a gift of *service* in the English language. To serve as a deacon is to represent God in a special way. To serve as a deacon means that the defense and service of God becomes a response to the prayer life that one undertakes in life. When God calls you in the world of prayer to go out and serve, then the role of the deacon makes sense to us. A deacon becomes a symbol to the life of service that each of us is called to live. When a deacon takes God's ministry to the hospitals and nursing homes, when he teaches the marriage and baptism classes, the deacon fulfills the command that the deacon assigns to him on the day of his ordination: "Believe what you read, teach what you believe and practice what you teach."

I was reflecting this week on the papal election that just took place in Rome and how the new Pope dressed in his white vestments for the first time. Tradition tells us that when the Pope dresses in these white garments the day of his election, he enters what has been called "The Weeping Room," the place where the new Holy Father realizes the immense responsibility that awaits him with his new duties. It is in this weeping room that this new Holy Father often cries, knowing that, like St. Stephen, the road he will walk will be a difficult one. In the past 100 years, you have had another Pope Benedict that had to get the Church through World War I, a Pope Pius that had to save the papal lands from an Italian dictator, another Pope Pius that had to save the Church from the Axis powers during World War II and a John Paul that kept a Church strong during the defeat of Communism in Eastern Europe. If any of us can realize the weight of this type of service, then no one here would be strong enough to endure the weight of that moment during that period of enlightenment.

Today is the day to realize that each one of us is called to the life of service. God has graced us in prayer and has led us to this altar so that our houses can be nourished by Christ's Body and Blood. We are commissioned at each Mass to go out to love and serve in God's name. Our prayer leads us to a life that a deacon symbolizes; it is up to us to decide whether we answer the call of God and follow the life of service or allow the houses of our faith to remain empty and devoid of God's presence.

I would like to conclude today's homily by offering a special blessing given to deacons on the day of his ordination. The prayer is geared towards a deacon's ministry, but in reality it applies to all of us who love and serve the Lord. This is how the prayer goes...

Lord, send forth upon (this person of service the gift of) the Holy Spirit, that he may be strengthened by the gift of your sevenfold grace to carry out faithfully the work of the ministry. May he excel in every virtue: in love that is sincere, in concern for the sick and the poor, in unassuming authority, in self-discipline and in holiness of life. May his conduct exemplify your commandments and lead your people to imitate his purity of life. May he remain strong and steadfast in Christ, giving to the world the witness of a pure conscience. May he in this life imitate your Son, who came, not to be served but to serve and one-day reign with him in heaven.[xxii]

May all of us desire to imitate our Lord by desiring to serve others rather than by being served by others. This is our prayer.

6th Sunday of Easter (Acts 8: 5-8, 14-17; Ps 66: 1-3, 4-5, 6-7, 16-20; 1 Pet 3: 15-18; John 14: 15-21)

During the early years of my priesthood, I had decided to invest my vacation time by touring the southern end of the diocese and getting to know the many "out of the way" parishes that make up the seven counties which our priests serve. Since I was raised in the country, I specifically wanted to experience the farm life of the diocese and the people who attend the local churches in Ford, Iroquois, Kankakee and Grundy counties. I have a strong belief that the country folk have a great need for priestly ministry and I personally feel the call to return back to my roots one day and offer them God's grace.

With this in mind, I took up an offer (about a decade ago) to cover for a priest in Gibson City, Illinois, Fr. Bill Smith. During the three weeks I spent down at his parish, I felt as if I were back in my hometown of Sandwich, Illinois, experiencing the farm lifestyle to which I was most accustomed during my formative years. Understanding the life of the farmer is a culture to itself; I had to recondition myself to think like a farmer, just like I would do the same if I were ministering to the Hispanic community, the faithful of DuPage County or some other group that goes about life in some unique type of way.

In the case of Gibson City, I entered a town with a population around 4000 folks and lived at the rectory of Our Lady of Lourdes Catholic Church that supported about 200 families. Gibson City is about a half an hour north of Champaign, IL right down Route 47 and is the home of a "Rock 'n Roll" McDonalds, *two* drive-in movie theaters and the best German Restaurant south of I-80.

In addition to spending time in this small farming community for those three weeks, I also had the opportunity to tour the rest of the parishes from down south, from Gilman to Paxton to Cabery to Wilton Center. I found out that our diocese supports a national shrine in St. Anne, Illinois and that in the city of Ashkum, the faithful still kneel at the communion rail to receive the Body of Christ.

I also had the chance to visit my favorite parish down south, St. Mary's Church in Beaverville, Illinois. If I had an actual aspiration left in life, I guess mine would be to become a bishop of one city and one city only – I want to be known as "the Bishop of Beaverville," where I can sit in a Cathedral that holds some 1200 people that serves a parish community made up if less than 100 families. I guess someone thought an airport or other place of commerce would be built in the area, so the faithful jumped the gun and built this huge church, which is now recognized as a national landmark. Sunday Masses are usually held in a wing of that that church, heated by space heaters during the winter (since the parish cannot afford to heat the entire church with such a small membership).

During my stay in Gibson City, I spent my evenings in the rectory of Our Lady of Lourdes' Church. During those three weeks, I got to know a little bit about the pastor, Fr. Bill Smith. Today's gospel talks about those who live the life of love and obedience being the ones who actually realize the presence of the Holy Spirit within them. Fr. Bill Smith seemed to me to be one of those people. Unless you were once a parishioner at St. Walter's Parish in Roselle or one of the other parishes which Fr. Smith served as pastor, I am guessing that no one in this church has ever heard of this particular cleric. Fr. Bill quietly served at Our Lady of Lourdes Parish for the last 20 years of his life, until he died at the parish in 2003. Every Sunday he would celebrate three Masses – one in Gibson City, one in the city of Melvin and one in Roberts, Illinois. Because he wanted to conserve parish finances, Fr. Smith celebrated daily Mass in his rectory basement with the fifteen or so faithful that came to worship. Unfortunately for me, the ceiling of the rectory basement was only six feet high and I am taller than that, so I had to celebrate Mass for three weeks with my legs in a semi-split position so that my head would not hit the tiles of the basement.

While serving in Gibson City, Fr. Bill did not take much of a salary and chose not to spend much money on himself. In fact, the parishioners became concerned about Fr. Smith's notorious frugality and the beater car that he drove, realizing that Fr. Bill would not invest his money in buying a new vehicle.

Due to their concerns, a group of parishioners put their resources together and ended up buying him a car that was actually safe to drive on the road. These parishioners loved their pastor and would extend themselves to the limit for the sake of his welfare.

About a decade ago, a family from Gibson City realized that their pastor had not taken a vacation in some seven years and, for his anniversary, invited him on a pilgrimage to his home country of Ireland. What I have not mentioned up until this point was that Fr. Bill was deeply Irish in his lifestyle. His entire rectory was a testimony to his native land, with every Gaelic symbol hanging on the wall and Irish papers sprawled all over the house, unreadable to the rest of us unless you spoke the native tongue. I learned more about this particular culture in the three weeks I lived down south than I had my entire life, up until I came became pastor at St. Patrick's in Joliet.

I also learned that as thick was his dedication to the Irish heritage, so thick also was the smoke on the windows of his rectory from the pipe that he had blown for those 20 years. During my time at the parish, I learned that *no one had cleaned the windows of the parish for all the years he lived in that house!* The first day I opened the dusty drapes to look through the windows, I realized that I could not see one thing on the outside from the inside. Thus, I dedicated some of my three weeks to a one-man rectory cleaning project at Our Lady of Lourdes only for the fact *that I wanted to breathe!*

As I read today's gospel, I connected the imagery that our Lord associated with the Holy Spirit with the type of life that Fr. Bill lived. I thought about the words that our Lord spoke in today's gospel and connected it to one of the commentaries attributed to this text (*The Jerome Biblical Commentary*). Here are the two passages in question:

> If you love me, you will keep my commandments. I will ask the Father and will give you another Advocate to be with you always, the Spirit of truth, whom the world cannot accept, because it neither sees nor knows him.

> (In the context of today's gospel,) the conditions of love and obedience that apply to the prayer for the Spirit (v. 16) are also required for the efficacy of any prayer (as pointed out in v. 13).[xxiii]

When I connected those dirty windows to the life of the Spirit, I began to think about my soul. Outside of our Lord and our Blessed Mother, the rest of us have souls that are stained with sin. Like cleaning my glasses each day and cleaning my room each week, unless I constantly clean my soul from the stain of sin, there is no way I can see the Holy Spirit within my house. Out of my love for God, I am obligated to clean first the window of faith that rests in my soul so that I metaphorically can see the presence of God in my life clearly. To receive communion with a stained soul is like trying to drive a vehicle with a dirty windshield – we become an accident waiting to happen.

Fr. Smith reminded me that a clean heart and a dedicated life allowed him to see this Holy Spirit within his heart and the reason why he became a priest for the Joliet Diocese. Concerning Fr. Smith's vocation, I came to a fitting conclusion about his life – clean soul, dirty windows. We all have those metaphorical dirty windows in life. How many times has God called each of us to our specific vocations, dirty windows and all, because God knows what lives inside the house called our lives and the goodness that has the potential to shine through it?

We have heard from the statistics that many Catholics in our community do not choose to clean their windows and recognize the presence of our Lord, either in their Catholic Churches or in many cases even in their own lives, *our* own lives. Many choose not to attend Mass on Sundays, even though the Third Commandment requires us to do so. Many do not go to reconciliation, even though this contradicts the second precept of the Church, especially when serious sin is involved. Many in our society choose to live their Catholic lives without cleaning their windshields before they drive. If we cannot see the God that is standing right in front of us, it is much more difficult to follow the example that God is setting in front of us as well.

Today's gospel sets the bar quite high for those in the faith – it requires us to be people committed to obedience and love. For those who follow this path, the presence of the Holy Spirit becomes very clear and the call of God becomes much more obvious to those who can see what God has in store for them.

May we all follow the path that Fr. Bill Smith set for the people of Our Lady of Lourdes Parish in Gibson City, IL. May we all become the windows to the Holy Spirit in the way we follow our Lord's guidance and serve each other in love. This is our prayer.

Ascension Sunday (Acts 1: 1-11; Ps 47: 2-3, 6-7, 8-9; Eph 1: 17-23; Mt 28: 16-20)

As I have preached many times over the last year, I try to make Saturday nights a sacred time for my family, an occasion to pull away from parish and other responsibilities in order to focus on an aspect of my life that is really important to me. The usual routine for our family get togethers involves eating dinner, catching up with our goings-on in life, solving the world's problems and then making sure I spend time with my much younger brother, who lives his life pouring over books and watching <u>Fox News</u>.

Sometimes I stay with the family for a few hours, leaving just before Julian's bedtime. When my brother was younger, my father insisted I stay with them to witness my brother's sacred ritual in which he participated each night before he went to bed.

So I stayed and lingered over my dessert while my brother took what seemed like an intolerably long time in the bath, which according to my schedule seemed interminable since a nine-year-old takes forever to get into the tub and then, once he settled in, to get *out* of the tub (nine year olds rarely make it easy when it comes to personal hygiene, I guess). After the bath, Julian headed for the bed to recite and share a litany of stories that were to his liking that particular evening, having to be shared both in Polish and in English. After the stories, Julian said his prayers, reciting the Our Father in a dialect that makes me think he was speaking in tongues. Then, after a quick kiss on the forehead, my father and his wife turned out the light and settle in for about 9-10

Rev. Peter G. Jankowski

hours of peaceful rest before the chaos began all over again the next day.

As I was reading today's gospel, I was thinking about that bedtime experience with my brother. For Julian, the first people and the last people he sees each day are the people on earth who love him the most, namely mom and dad. They are his security and his strength, the ones he tests quite often but the one to whom he turns for most problems of life. I was thinking as I was younger that there was a great deal of comfort hearing my own mother's voice as the last one at night, something I could take to sleep with me, knowing everything was going to be all right during the nighttime hours.

The best way I can describe this very unique gospel from Matthew (not found in the other gospels) is one where Jesus is giving words of comfort to a group of men before he departs for the night. Church theologians will give us all kinds of fancy explanations to what is going on. They will tell us that in this mountain experience, we recall how Moses felt God's presence at Mt. Sinai when he received the Ten Commandments and how Jesus revealed God's presence during the transfiguration. Other theologians will tell us that in these words of Jesus, the Lord reveals Himself as the Alpha and the Omega (show the symbols found on the Sacramentary), the beginning and the end. Scripture scholars tell us this reading might very well be a fulfillment of the Book of Daniel, chapter seven, where it is written, "The ancient one took his throne. His clothing was snow bright and the hair on his head as white as wool."[xxiv] Still others will tell us that this event on the mountain is a great *Parousia* that has revealed to us to end time of the world and what awaits us on the last day.

As much as all these things are true, as is with all those great theological theophanies, the image that I associate with this gospel passage is this: that Jesus will be with all of us until the end of the age, that when we follow the Lord and live out His commands, that Jesus will love us and be with us always.

After these words, Jesus ascends to heaven and takes His place at the right hand of the Father. But like a father and mother who tuck a child in at the end of a night, Jesus has not abandoned us; is still with us. For those who understand, we are not afraid because our Savior is by our side, is in the next room and is a prayer away for anyone who takes time actually to pray. As we walk this faith journey, we are never far away from our parents and we are not far away from God. It is those words, "I am with you always," that give me and hopefully you, a sense of comfort as we go through the day.

Today is a day to remember and to give thanks. Today is a day to keep our mothers and fathers close to our hearts as much as we keep the love of our Lord's. May we all follow Christ's command to spread the gospel message throughout the world so that we, too, can experience the response that Christ offers to those who believe: *Know I am with you always, until the end of the age* (Mt 28: 20). This is our prayer.

Rev. Peter G. Jankowski

Pentecost Sunday (Acts 2: 1-11; Ps 104: 1-24, 29-30, 31-34; 1 Cor 12: 3b-7, 12-13; John 20: 19-23)

There is a tradition in the Catholic Church that we customarily offer at the end of the Easter Season that I would like to highlight today. The tradition states that on the last day of Easter, namely Pentecost Sunday that the Easter Candle be processed out of Church at the end of the liturgy and placed near the baptismal font to symbolize the conclusion of the Easter Season.

If you recall, at the first night of this season, on the Easter Vigil, the entire church was darkened except for this one light that burned fifty days ago. This was the light of hope that reminded us no matter how desperate our lives may be, that this light of God would always lead us to heaven. It has burned for fifty days during our church services and following today, it will be displayed next to the baptismal font, where we will continue to light it during baptismal services. On occasion, we return the candle to the front of the church to commemorate funerals of our baptized faithful as well.

For the purposes of today's homily, I would like to focus on that Easter light, the one that we will extinguish at the conclusion of today's Mass. The symbol of fire plays many roles in the scriptures. In the Old Testament, Elijah carried this fire of God's spirit from Mt. Carmel down to the people who wished visibly to encounter their Lord. In the Book of Daniel, King Nebuchadnezzar attempted to throw Shadrach, Meshach and Abednego into a red-hot fire, only to see three men purified by the head and to have seen the Son of God present in their midst.

In the Acts of the Apostles' reading for today, we read how the Spirit enflamed the mouths of the apostles with "tongues of fire," an image only found in this particular reading. In the early Church, fire was seen as a means by which the soul was cleansed from sin, purified clean so to enter the kingdom of heaven.

As I read today's scripture passages and reflected on this image of the Holy Spirit as fire, I came to the conclusion that the symbols attributed to this flame have just about the same import as that of water. Fire can bring us life and fire can bring us death.

Let's start with death. If we choose to allow fire to kill us, then we will be easily consumed by it. In our society, there are many things that turn us away from love so as to consume us. Sometimes the media focuses on fear and loathe rather than love. Gossip, envy, pride, lust, all those things can consume us like fire and can turn us away from the ultimate goodness. When the symbol of fire consumes the hearts of those who give in to loathe and violence, most all of us can attest to the results of such hatred.

But fire can also purify and cleanse us. When we choose to follow God, we are filled with grace and made clean so that no matter what happens in the world, we will always be warmed by the glow of God's presence and purified of those things that bear us down. No matter how bad other individuals may act in the world, the flame of God will not be quenched within our own lives.

As I have watched the news like you over the last weeks, we all have realized that so much conflict and division take place that is in such need of purification. It is up to us to decide whether we want to be purified by fire or destroyed by us. As St. Paul writes in 1 Thessalonians 5, we must resist the temptation to allow this fire of God's spirit to be quenched by the things around us. In the end, our salvation is not dependent on whether the person next to us has sinned or not. Our salvation depends on whether <u>we</u> choose to sin or to be cleansed from sin.

As we find out on this last day of the Easter Season, the Easter Candle will be extinguished, but the flame continues to glow within us, as long as we choose to believe. We will use the symbols of the Spirit at this Mass – the incense, the water, the fire – but it is now our responsibility to hold these images close in our heart so that they remain within us. When we do so, the season of Easter becomes an everlasting one. If not, we remain stuck in the season of Lent and Penance, continually engulfed by the negative image of fire, a flame that eats away at us like the fear and anger it feeds off.

My challenge to all of you (for all of us) is to ask how you have kept that flame burning throughout the season. Have we continually loved those around us? Have we sacrificed for others as Christ has sacrificed for us? They key to the Easter mystery is to hold that mystery in our heart so that we do not forget. When we hold it tightly, this presence of Christ will not go away – it remains an eternal light unquenched by the scandals of the world.

I invite you to follow me out of church today as we carry our light throughout the world. May we make that light present in everything we do as we fill our hearts with God's spirit and share that spirit with the people that we meet. This is our prayer.

Stories on the Journey: The Season of Ordinary Time (Cycle A Homilies)

2nd Sunday in Ordinary Time (Is 49: 3, 5-6; Ps 40: 2-4, 7-8a, 8b-9, 10; 1 Cor 1: 1-3; John 1: 29-34)

Why do we need a Church?
As some of you may be aware, in addition to my pastoral responsibilities here at the parish, I also teach two courses each semester at the University of St. Francis. In the fall, I am honored to teach an online course on the Old Testament and am blessed to teach the students about the religions of the world, touring the various places of worship throughout the area. In the winter semester, I teach an online course on the New Testament while rotating courses with the students in class on Church History and Social Justice. I also teach online courses for Dayton University for students living throughout the world.

Concerning the latter, I am blessed to teach at Dayton, assisting catechists and church leaders in their formation and growth in their prayer life. I have taught students both in the states and those who live in military bases throughout the world. Students have enrolled in these courses from England, Japan, South Africa and everywhere in between. Many of the students have little to no experience with the Catholic faith, taking their first steps on this faith journey. Many of the students have never really engaged in a theological discussion before.

This being the first week of the course, we began our time together by asking some of the basic questions concerning the faith: *How do we know that God exists? Why did God create the universe? Why does God permit evil in the world?* The question with which we started this homily, *Why do we need a Church?*

The students engage in this conversation through daily blogs and online conversation. I was inspired by a series of these blogs last week concerning this subject that I would like to share with you.

> Of this topic, Linda first writes, "A Christian without a church family is an orphan. Life is hard and has many hard choices. It is great to have a church community to guide you in making those choices."
>
> Nancy responds by saying, "Having a church seems like it can be very comforting for people who are involved. I can see how a church can seem like a family and that without it you can feel orphaned."
>
> Pamela provides an intense entry to this discussion: "I have a friend that lost her teenage daughter to suicide and my friend received tremendous support and strength from her church family. It touched me to watch God's people comfort this woman with so many godly words of love. The outpouring of love was a healing force. My friend later told me that she didn't have thoughts of leaving the church during this crisis, conversely, she grew stronger in the church and knew that the love of God and His followers would help her through this horrible time.
>
> It has been five years now and my friend still receives cards and phone calls from church members asking how she is doing during a holiday,

etc... Yes, the church is a family and the best friendships are developed with Christ in the middle."

A student named Shawnda provides the inspiration to my homily with her entry: "When I hear someone mention how they don't feel it's necessary to attend a church to have fellowship with God, I immediately refer them to the scripture Hebrews 10: 24-25 which states, *'We must consider how to rouse one another to love and good works. We should not stay away from our assembly, as is the custom of some, but encourage one another and this all the more as you see the day drawing near.'* I believe this scripture kind of sums up the reason we need a church."

Now I suppose I can go all theological on you and explain the ecclesiological significance of the cross that hangs over our altar. I can tell you how after Jesus' death, according to the 19th Chapter of St. John's Gospel, a nearby soldier thrust a lance upon our Lord's side, from which both blood and water poured out. According to one commentary from The New American Bible, the blood and water may have symbolized both sacraments of the Eucharist and baptism. In the world of Ecclesiology (or the Church), Church theologians will tell us that the blood pouring from Jesus' side symbolizes God while the water from His side symbolizes humanity. Theologians will tell us that the comingling of blood and water symbolizes the first Christian marriage between our Lord and His bride, the Church.

According to many theologians, through this act the Catholic Church was born. St. Athanasius (296-373) will write that every time the celebrant pours a little water into the wine during the offertory prayers, as he writes, "God became man, so that man might become like God."[xxv] Mother Church validates this teaching with the offertory prayer at Mass that is attributed to St. Athanasius: *Through the mingling of this water and wine, may we come to share the divinity of Christ who humbled Himself to share in our humanity.*

In the world of ecclesiology, we learn that Christ the groom shows us how willing is to sacrifice His own life to protect His bride, the Church. We are taught that this sacrifice was made to unite us and to protect us, so that those who are covered under His protection of love are kept safe from the poison of sin. We are taught that the bride that our Lord married is *not* this building. As cherished as this worship space is for us who pray in it, this space could be destroyed tomorrow in a blink of an eye, but as long as two or more of the faithful continue to carry on the mission of Christ's love, always in God's name, the Church remains strong and vibrant (Mt 18: 20).

We certainly are taught these lessons in the scripture readings we just proclaimed at today's liturgy. The first reading from Isaiah pines for a messiah to restore a separated people who fell due to perpetual sin, a messiah who would come to restore the former glory of one Israel. Our second reading from Paul's First Letter to the Corinthians laments over the loss of those who have fallen away from the faith but challenges the faithful not to condemn the fallen away. Rather, St. Paul encourages the faithful to learn the lesson about why the fallen have left the Church and to avoid the pitfalls of this way of life. The saint implores the faithful to hold fast together as members of the same body, with Christ as the head. In today's gospel, St. John the Baptist reveals this Jesus as the Christ, the Messiah who has come to restore the fallen nation of Israel and that the power of the Holy Spirit serves as the great uniter and healer that makes us one.

All these themes point to a united Catholic Church that focuses on the "we" instead of the "I" (to use a sports' analogy here, there certainly is no "I" in team in the case of the Church). Because of Christ's sacrifice, no faithful Christian is left behind; no one is left an orphan. In the faith of the Church, all believers are sacred, all human beings are sacred and when we love them in God's name, no matter the color of their skin or their way of life, we then learn to love God and understand better the understanding of Church.

None of you are orphans – all of you are special. All of you make up the members of the body of Christ. May you realize how important you are to us and may you and I make sure that all in this community feel the same way. Let us share that brotherly/sisterly love with the people that we meet. This is our prayer.

For more information about the online program at the University of Dayton, please check out https://vlcff.udayton.edu/.

3rd Sunday in Ordinary Time (Is 8: 23b—9: 3; Ps 27: 1, 4, 13-14; 1 Cor 1: 10-13, 17; Mt 4: 12-23 or 4: 12-17)

This might be the only time as a Catholic priest that I can preach about incandescent light. The lighting industry is moving away from this specific technology; the government has passed laws to forbid it. In fact, because of events that transpired at the parish, my studies this week required me to learn about incandescent light bulbs, fluorescent light bulbs and LED light bulbs, subjects no theologian I know has ever discussed.

The subject of the light bulb became prominent in my life on the Sunday before Christmas. I was checking the buildings at night when I ended up falling down by the outdoor chapel stairway in between the Church and the rectory. Because all the incandescent light bulbs were burned out on that part of the property early in the fall season and because the weather was not conducive to changing the bulbs, we went without lights for a few weeks until my pre-Christmas accident. It seems that whoever installed the light fixtures on that part of the campus set them up in such a way that you would have to stand on the top of a freestanding ladder or build a riser in order to change the lights, something that is not easily accomplished during the coldest, snowiest days of the year.

The day after the fall, our maintenance man replaced the bulbs on a more moderate day of winter but not before he, my office manager and I had what my father calls a "philosophical discussion" on the function of a light bulb, more specifically the *cost* of a light bulb. At our pre-Christmas meeting, Jim taught us about the differences between incandescent light bulbs, fluorescent lights and LED lights. It was that day I was taught that the incandescent light bulb, the cheapest variety of lighting fixtures and the one about we are the most accustomed to use, provide the least amount of light and were prone to burning out much quicker than other fixtures.

At the parish, we slowly have been changing our bulbs from incandescent bulbs to the fluorescent ones, anyway. You can recognize these new fluorescent lights as the spirally ones now sold in most hardware stores. If you believe Wikipedia (http: //en.wikipedia.org/wiki/Fluorescent_lamp), fluorescent bulbs are about four times more expensive than incandescent light bulbs ($1.50 per bulb as opposed to $.40 per) but last about 9-10 times longer than the cheaper light version (based on normal usage) and use less energy. Thus, the initial cost of fluorescent lights is higher than the incandescent but ultimately is more cost effective down the line.

Concerning lighting products, the preference for our maintenance staff is to use LED bulbs. Unfortunately, in today's age, a typical LED light costs significantly more than either an incandescent or fluorescent one but lasts, on normal usage, for up to 23 years.[xxvi] Because an LED light burns so little energy, they are, by far, the most cost effective lights on the market but initially (and significantly) the most expensive.

(There are other options on the market, but for the sake of this homily, I would like to stay with the three options that I have cited today.)

So how do we solve this problem? Do we follow the advice of our office manager, who tells us we need to spend frugally because our parish does not have the resources to invest in such expensive light fixtures? Do we follow the advice of the maintenance man, who explains that the high cost of the bulbs today will more offset by the significantly cheaper costs of electrical use and replacement down the line? Do we wait until the cost of LED lights become more affordable for us to spend? Most importantly, this pastor and preacher asks why he just spent the last five minutes giving you a comparison/contrast on our spending practices which seemingly has nothing to do with our scripture readings today?

The reason for such a long winded explanation is that I realized this last week how the faith life in our society very much parallels the discussion of lighting fixtures at the parish. We probably know of those few who invest their lives in the faith in the same way we purchase LED lights – these people make a heavy investment in the faith that is often costly to them. These are the people that stand up to live the faith of Christ, knowing full well the repercussions of such a lifestyle that they choose to live. The fifth chapter of Matthew's gospel very much defines the type of reward that awaits those who suffer the gospel of Christ: *Blessed are you when they insult you and persecute you and utter every kind of evil against you falsely because of me. Rejoice and be glad because your reward will be great in heaven.*[xxvii]

Then there are those who are like the fluorescent light bulb. These good folks are devoted to the faith – they attend Mass weekly, they follow the commandments more or less and they pretty much follow the teachings of the faith as a general rule. Their investment in the faith needs to be checked on occasion and every so often the bulb burns out and there is a slip and fall along the way, the faithful person on the fluorescent path keeps that light burning with good regularity.

Then there is the incandescent light bulb. This is the functional person – the ones who comes to church on occasion and knows the requisite prayers that were taught them. Depending on the wattage, those at this level might feel that going through the motions is sufficient enough for their salvation but the bulb is often dim in their life and often needs to be replaced or recharged. At this level, the investment in the light is certainly not greater than those whose initial investment brings higher dividends.

Then there are those who choose to live in the darkness. For these people, there is no desire to live in the light but would rather just live in darkness than make any investment at all. For them, faith is a waste of time and the desires of hedonism and worldly wants suppress any doctrines set forth by faith institutions.

I am sure that someone could make better analogies between the faith life and lighting fixtures, but I think you get the point. My purpose in this analogy is not to say that those who are most invested in the life of faith have earned a better chance at heaven than those who don't. My purpose is to say that some people choose to answer God's call with more conviction than others. In our first reading today, the Prophet Isaiah warns the chosen people that they have not invested much in the covenant of faith they made with our Lord and God. His warning in the early chapters of this book of the darkness that awaits is tempered by the hope of a light that will guide those with faith to the path of love that will draw the believer to the life of God.

Using that same example from Isaiah, our Lord in today's gospel also alludes to the light, reminding the believer of the light that has come to the world that will not fade, that will not be corrupted, a light that, if one chooses to embrace and follow, will draw them to an eternal life of peace symbolized by this glowing presence.

The choice set before us is a simple one – how do we wish to equip our houses with light? In the earthly realm, do we wish initially to spend a good deal of money with cost-effective lighting that will pay dividends in the long run? Can we afford this? In the heavenly realm, do we wish to make that initial investment in the faith that, if carried throughout our lives, will lead up to this symbolic perpetual light that will keep us warm and safe perpetually? Or do we just not care or choose not to make any investment in faith at all, preferring to live in the darkness than doing any work in building a relationship with the divine?

Our Lord has provided us with the spiritual tools to make whichever decision we choose to make. Let us make this choice well as we allow this light to shine in our lives so that we may share this light with the people that we meet. This is our prayer.

Rev. Peter G. Jankowski

4th Sunday in Ordinary Time (Zeph 2: 3; 3: 12-13; Ps 146: 6c-7, 8-9a, 9b-10; 1 Cor 1: 26-31; Mt 5: 1-12a)

... And blessed are the (Super Bowl Underdogs), for they shall win the Super Bowl. How many of you are going to watch the Super Bowl? As usual, there is a lot of hype to "Super Bowl Sunday." On this day, you will see some of the best commercials that television has to offer. You will see the best graphics, the best analysis. As for the game itself, many of you probably think that the favored team is going to walk all over the underdog team (which is usually the case) and some of you could care less about the football game altogether.

Yet, it seems that the one thing that this game usually has to offer is a David and Goliath story, where one team is dominant though many people cheer for the underdog to win. Many hope that someone with the odds against them will overcome all adversities and do well. We all hope that good things come out of hopeless situations. Lord knows, I have been a Cub fan all my life – I am an expert when it comes to hopeless situations.

Today's gospel roots for the underdog. In fact, the entire bible is a bible for the underdog. Whether we read about Job overcoming insurmountable problems to find peace with God or Jonah making it out of a big fish in order to preach about God, the Bible offers many stories about people who overcome the odds and make well in life. We read in the book of Job a story about God's conversation with the devil and whether the devil could corrupt a wealthy man to such a degree that the wealthy man would turn away from God. As Job is stripped of his family, his wealth and his health, chapter after chapter he argues bitterly with God, pleading as to why the Lord of all goodness would allow something this horrible to happen to him. God's response to Job was to stay the course and have faith. It was because of Job's faith that God rewarded him with more than he could ever imagine. What Job received on earth is the gift of salvation that all who stay the course will receive in heaven.

A week or so ago, the Church celebrated the feast of the Conversion of St. Paul, a man who used to kill Christians for a living, who lived a life so contrary to what we believe. Even with this knowledge, God chose *this* particular individual to be a witness of faith for us. God chose one of the weakest of humans so that we could see how even the weakest of humans could become a disciple of God. What a great hope this offers us in our life – *everyone, no matter how good or bad they may seem in life, has a chance to meet God face-to face.*

The Bible shows us about this God who can do all and yet chooses to enter this frail body and go through an experience that none of us would want to have. Yet, did it for us. This God who can do all ended up being reduced to nothing, beyond nothing and in the process opened the doors for all Pauls and Jobs in the world so that they, too, could have a chance to see God in their lives again. From God's example, we learn that <u>nothing</u> becomes insurmountable with Him at our side. Therefore, we must conclude that God, today, must be a fan of the underdog (well, sort of).

Rev. Peter G. Jankowski

Today's gospel begins a section in Matthew that we call the "Sermon of the Mount." Here, Jesus teaches how to follow His example by following a few basic practices of our faith. In essence, Jesus tells us how to cop an attitude, a "be" attitude. tells us that the way to God is to be humble, to be poor in spirit and to be sorrowing. When we care for others, even when the day is long and we have other things to do, we "be" this attitude. When we live a God-like life by offering our time to others for the sake of God, even when others insult us and persecute us because of our beliefs, we are blessed indeed. In the process, we have copped the attitude.

The key in reaching God is through our humility, or in bible-language, to become poor in spirit, to become the lowest born. St. Paul writes today that "God chose the lowly and despised of the world, those who count for nothing, to reduce to nothing those who are something, so that no human being might boast before God."[xxviii] In order to be something with God, we strive to be nothing. Now that's sounds bizarre, but that's what it means to be poor in spirit.

Yes, the Super Bowl is a big day in the world of sports. I'm sure there will be lots of parties, lots of food. I myself prefer a big pot of flaming-hot Texas chili which will probably be more exciting than the game itself. So while we're watching this game or doing whatever, let's cheer for the underdog, even if it's symbolic. Let's see what this team represents symbolically as a reminder of the humble people in the world who sacrifice themselves on a daily basis for the sake of others. Let's try to reflect this same type of sacrificial life by living a humble, blessed, life. In other words, let's cop this particular attitude and bring it to the altar today. This is our prayer.

5th Sunday in Ordinary Time (Is 58: 7-10; Ps 112: 4-5, 6-7, 8-9; 1 Cor 2: 1-5; Mt 5: 13-16)

How many of you like hot dogs? Where are your favorite places? Some people in my community like the dollar hot dogs from a place called "Babes"; others are partial to the chain restaurant, "Portillo's." I myself am partial to a hotdog done "Maxwell Street"-style, a bratwurst served with lots of mustard and sautéed onions. The people from the A&W food chain like to make their dogs "Coney Island"-style, with lots of chili and onions served on top. There's the famous "Chicago-style" hotdog that is loaded with anything you can find... except ketchup. For me, Toronto has great grilled hot dogs by side-street venders. At Navy Pier in Chicago, there even is a place where you can buy hot dogs prepared like they would from different parts of the country.

However, as of late my favorite hotdogs come from a low grade place in Joliet called "Joe's," located at the six-corner intersection of town. To be honest, the hot dog place in Joliet is a dive. The signs are hand-written, the place could use a paint job and you don't exactly go to Joe's for the ambiance. But the dogs are great. The fries that come with the dogs are the best in the city – the grease seep from the fries so deeply that you can see the stains come through on the outside of the bag that contains them.

The best part about Joe's hot dogs, for me, is the sign that is taped right by the cash register that defines the kind of product they serve. The sign is a faithful person's dream and a doctor's nightmare - The sign reads and I quote, "WE SALT EVERYTHING!" I love that sign! I love salt! Whenever I read this notice, I dream lovingly of my arteries blocking up with every bite of the dog, with those fries drenched salty, grease-stained goodness. For my money (what little I have!), the more salt and grease you have, the better off you are. Salt is a good thing; bad for the blood pressure, but essential for the soul.

In the world of faith, salt plays an extremely important part within Bible literature. In the 19th Chapter of the Book of Genesis, Lot's wife had a momentary loss of faith and as a result was turned into a pillar of salt. In Leviticus and Ezekiel, salt was a symbolic offering given to sacrificial victims. In the Book of Judges, salt was thrown upon a city that was destroyed as a sign of conquest. A "Salt Land" is also called a "desert wasteland" in Deuteronomy and Ezekiel calls the bitter waters by the Dead Sea as a source for salt.

However, in the Old Testament, salt was also a symbol for friendship. Salt was the symbol that signified a type of covenant or friendship between one party and another. In today's society, there is a tradition in some cultures to pass salt to a neighbor as a sign of respect and love. The idea here is that salt enhances the flavor of a friendship, thus making the salt an essential ingredient for growth.

When we are called to be "the salt of the earth" in today's gospel, it is not just a nice metaphor with which we walk away. As the disciples are called to carry this gospel message out to the nations, so we are called to do the same. The Second Vatican Council made this clear in their document *Lumen Gentium* by writing that

> The laity are called in a special way to make the Church present and operative in those places and circumstances where only through them can it become the salt of the earth. Thus every layman, in virtue of the very gifts bestowed upon Him, is at the same time a witness and a living instrument of the mission of the Church itself "according to the measure of Christ's bestowal."[xxix]

It is the responsibility of the laity, the religious and the clergy to spread this gospel message, to pass the salt, to build friendships and to reveal Christ to the world.

Let us all learn of the gift of passing this salt of faith. Let us pass on the teachings of Christ and set the example of this faith by living the faith for those around us. We are called to live out this faith for the sake of the children in this congregation, to share the stories of Jesus with those around us because those stories of Jesus make this whole journey possible.

We are all called to pass on this faith because *you are* the salt of the earth. We all are. Let us never conceal or refrain from sharing this gift. Let us continue to share the stories of our faith which gives the flavor of love to those around us. This is our prayer.

6th Sunday in Ordinary Time (Sir 15: 16-21; Ps 119: 1-2, 4-5, 17-18, 33-34; 1 Cor 2: 6-10; Mt 5: 17-37 or 5: 20-22a, 27-28, 33-34a, 37)

Have you ever heard the phrase, "I need my space," or "I need to find myself," or something similar? We all need space, a place that we consider sacred. In this space, you feel safe, you feel comfortable, you feel protected and you never feel lonely. Sometimes we don't realize we have that space, but it is always there. We just need to see it. In the house, this space may be in a bedroom or in the kitchen. At work, it may be an office. In this country, it may be your house. In Church, it may be in the presence of other Christians. Each of us needs our space.

But we also learn that in order to have this space, we need rules in which this space can be found. How can members of a family live together if each person in the family cannot respect their brothers and sisters, or how can Christians be with God if they don't build a relationship with God?

When we have this space, we have what St. Paul calls "freedom," not just a choice between doing something or not doing something, but a freedom to live with God in a safe place, a place where we can freely receive the grace of God without anyone taking that grace. When we walk outside our rooms our homes and feel safe wherever we go, we have found this freedom.

In this Church, we are given space as well. God offered this space to us in Old Testament times and people were introduced to God in the process. The chosen people learned the rules of God that allowed them to live in this space. When people did not follow the rules, God punished them and the people lost the space. As time passed, many people forgot who this God was that created the rules, so God came down to meet us. Today's Gospel introduces us to the person who gave us the rules, who gave us the life.

God presents us these rules today in a form scholars call "The Antitheses." For instance, you might notice in today's gospel that Christ often states, "You have heard the commandment or the Old Testament say (this), but I say to you this." We heard this pattern in last week's gospel. From this pattern, we learn that our God has come down on earth not to just give rules but to fulfill them; is not a rule-maker but the rule Himself. The Old Testament gives us a set of rules to follow. The New Testament gives us a _life_ to follow, Christ's life, a life greater than anything that we have ever seen. People no longer became afraid of God in the sense of the Old Testament, but gained a great faith in God that drew them closer to God. By us following this same path of Christ, we recognize the limits of the space, we provide this huge area in which we spend time with God. How many times do we not appreciate the space that God, our families, or our country offers us? When we completely open our hearts to the love of God, then God becomes present to us. This presence is called "grace," and we all get it when we follow the rules that Christ set forth, when we follow the life that Christ set forth. With Christ, we learn that it is hard to live a Christian life, but the rewards are infinitely more than what we put into our faith... and we become blessed.

Today's challenge is to discipline ourselves to follow the rules. When we follow the rules of the family life, we make it possible to get along with everyone in the family. When we make peace with our brothers and sisters in this community, when a person strikes us on one cheek and we turn and offer this person your other cheek instead of fighting, when we can learn to love our enemies and all those who live around us, essentially when we live the Christian lifestyle that Christ set out for us to live, we find this space with God. This space allows us to receive God's grace. This space is our comfort, our support, a place where we never live alone. This space becomes God's kingdom in our midst. When we find the space, we are blessed more than anything else on earth.

Today and every day, let's live within the rules. Let's recognize the space of God in our lives. Let's let God offer us His grace within this space. Most importantly, let's offer this space to others in everything that we do. This is our prayer today.

7th Sunday in Ordinary Time (Lev 19: 1-2, 17-18; Ps 103: 1-2, 3-4, 8-10, 12-13; 1 Cor 3: 16-23; Mt 5: 38-48)

About ten years ago, I was serving as an Associate Pastor in one of the more affluent parishes in the diocese. In this particular assignment, we pretty much took care of ourselves in matters of cooking and cleaning and we learned very quickly the maintenance skills necessary to keep a parish running. For the more serious problems at our facility we would depend on the generosity of volunteers or paid professionals to solve the troubles that we encountered, from broken doors to leaky furnaces to things of that nature.

One Easter Night some ten years ago after all the services had concluded, I was alone in the house taking a long post Triduum nap. While sleeping, I started to hear a piercing sound all around me, a constant buzz that would not go away. *The sound was driving me crazy!!!* Up the stairs, down the stairs and throughout the house, I could not shake the buzz in my ear - this perpetual tone would not go away. After a while, I started to think that I had caused something to happen in the rectory, even though no candle was lit, no stove was turned on and I had been sleeping for quite a while. In my mind, all I could think about was a pastor returning back from his Easter Supper only to find his parish in a heap of ash.

I could not take the sound anymore so I called a volunteer at the parish named John to help me search the house for the problem. Now John was a married man with a family who left his own Easter festivities to help me stop this piercing noise. In the process, we spent a good twenty minutes together on a Sunday night looking for the source of this perpetual sound without any success. Eventually, John gave up on this search, telling me he had to return back home to celebrate Easter with his wife and kids.

Dejected that he could not help me solve this seemingly important issue, John picked up his coat and went for the door. It was then that a great moment of insight had presented itself to my friend.

As he was moving away from me, John noticed that the piercing noise within the house was becoming softer and softer while he was *moving away from me*. As he turned around and came closer to me, the sound grew louder and louder for him. He concluded that the sound was not coming from the house... *but from my pants' pocket.*

We emptied my pockets and located the culprit, an electric guitar tuner that perpetually plays a tuning note until you manually turn it off (I must have accidentally hit the "on" switch while I was sleeping). Needless to say, John never let me live that experience down and had a great story to take home to his family. Now I bring this story to you so the abuse can start all over again...

After reflecting on our gospel readings for this weekend, I started playing "The Name Game" with all the Johns with whom I have crossed paths in life. How many people named "John" have I served? How many people named John have served me? How many people named John have I offended? How many people named John have offended me? From what background does each person named "John" come and what talents and gifts do they possess? (By the way, you can play this "game" with any name you wish, whether it be John or Jim or Ben or Michael or Rebecca or Linda or Jane or Jill.)

I came to realize that I have crossed paths with people named "John" who were neighbors of mine when I was growing up and classmates that went to school with me during the various points of my education. People named John have taught me, have served me, have befriended me and have loved me. Some people named John have had difficulties with me as I have had with them. I came to reflect upon the people named John I befriended and asked myself a simple question – have I treated all of them, the ones I have liked and the ones with whom I have difficulty, as well as I treated my friend John in Aurora, IL?

We have been reading the last two weeks about the manner of conduct a good follower of Christ should live, as taught to us by the Lord's "Sermon on the Mount," specifically what scripture scholars call "The Six Antitheses" ("People say this but I say to you this"). The message of the text is simple – unless we love each person named John or Jane or whomever as we would as if they were our friend or beloved member of our family, then we have a long way to go before we can reach the kingdom of heaven.

Specifically, in this passage from the gospel of Matthew, we are called not to live like our society does with their type of "eye for an eye" mentality. The type of lifestyle depicted in today's gospel is described by scripture scholars as a *Lex Talionis,* so to speak, or *The Law of Retaliation.* This ancient practice has its origins in the Old Testament Law, as the Torah (or the first five books of the Old Testament) cite the use of this type of punishment at least three times in its writings: (Ex. 21: 23, 24; Lev. 24: 19, 20; and Deut. 19: 21). A similar law is found in the ancient Mesopotamian code of Hammurabi which replaced financial compensation for bodily injuries with physical injury for physical injury. The Old Testament understanding of the *Lex Talionis* was a person's offense against the covenant community was also an offense against the God of the covenant and would be dealt with in a manner equivalent to the crime.

This week, I ask you to think about the manner in which you wish to show God how important God is in our life by responding to His call to serve one another out of love so that every "John" encounter becomes a sacred one. May the voice of God speak in our hearts as if upon the mountain of faith, directing us in the manner which we treat our neighbors and all people around us. This is how shed the Lex Talionis mentality from our lives of faith and replace that law of retaliation with the *Lex Caritatis* or the law of love. Let us share this love with the people that we meet. This is our prayer.

8th Sunday in Ordinary Time A (Is 49: 14-15; Ps 62: 2-3, 6-7, 8-9; 1 Cor 4: 1-5; Mt 6: 24-34)

The inspiration for today's homily comes from two simple Latin words that most on this ship might remember, the response to which will make all the difference in the world. The words are these:

Dominus vobiscum. *R/. Et cum spiritu tuo.*
El Señor esté con Ustedes. *R/. Y con tu espíritu.*

As you know, November 27, 2011 and the First Sunday of Advent saw the English speaking Church throughout the world changing to a new translation of the liturgy that has been intact for a good twenty to thirty years. The English speaking bishops throughout the world thought the new translation was necessary; they wanted the English language not only to provide a more accurate translation from the original Latin but to also be utilized the same way throughout the world. The translation is unique in that the text we use in the United States will be the same text used in England, South Africa, Australia and all other countries where the English liturgy is celebrated.

One of the most significant changes in the text arises from the response of the Latin phrase, *Dominus vobiscum* or *The Lord be with you*. For most every other language group who prays the Mass in the vernacular, their response corresponds to the Latin phrase *Et cum spiritu tuo,* or in English *and with your spirit*. Ours was one of the few languages that return the welcoming gesture not to the Spirit within the person but to the person who was the vessel to the Spirit.

For me as a priest, this distinction is very important. When I celebrate this Mass and I am living my ministry correctly, I am hoping that you are not paying attention to "Pete Jankowski, the human being" who celebrates the Mass. If I am living my ministry correctly, you are paying attention primarily to the type of spirit and the presence of Christ that shines *through* Pete Jankowski the human being so that the grace you receive is not Pete Jankowski's grace but that of the Lord.

The problem I have as "Pete Jankowski" is that I worry about too many things in life. I have been conditioned that way – take away my guilt and worry and I wouldn't know what to do as a Catholic. So I worry. Like many of you, I take a break from the home life, although I still look back wondering how the bills are getting paid or whether things that need to get done will get done. Like many of you with children, I concern myself with how my children will behave outside of the Father's protection and whether me being there at the parish or not will make a difference.

I also worry because I am a sinner. As all of us human beings (save two) have walked the face of the earth with the pains of sin, I wonder how I can overcome those burdens that have prevented me from seeing my Lord clearly. Without the Lord's help, I stumble and fall; with God's help, everything is possible.

After doing a quick scan within *The New American Bible*, I came to find the theme or worry or anxiety rearing its ugly head just under two dozen times within those seventy-three books, mostly within the pages of the New Testament. You can find the passage we read today about worry in the first three gospels of the New Testament (see Mt 6: 24-32, Mk 13: 9-13 & Lk 12: 10-12). Our Lord offers a metaphor about worry in these three gospels as well, likening worry or anxiety to thorns in a garden which choke the seeds of faith that we plant, prohibiting them to grow (see Mt 13: 18-23, Mk 4: 3-20 and Lk 8: 4-15). Quite famously, our Lord remonstrates the busy St. Martha in the tenth chapter of Luke's gospel (vss. 38-42) for putting work ahead of her sister Mary's gazing prayer of faith.

As I see myself, as I see all of us, as living at times a life parallel to Martha and the thorns in the garden, I came to the realization once again that unless I empty myself of pride and vanity so that I may focus myself on that eternal gaze of the Lord, I am utterly lost. If I allow the Holy Spirit to work within me, though – if I live myself as a vessel of the Holy Spirit so that the spirit within me is full of God's grace and not of temptation and sin, it is then that I find peace within my life and my purpose. It is then that the phrase "and with your Spirit" becomes more than fitting for the life I live.

In this light, I came to find that the summary offered in the twelfth chapter of St. Luke's gospel serves me well, both as a priest and as a homilist:

> When they take you before synagogues and before rulers and authorities, do not worry about how or what your defense will be or about what you are to say. For the Holy Spirit will teach you at that moment what you should say.[xxx]

In this light, I found that the reading from the fourth chapter of St. Paul's Letter to the Philippians help to the cause of my priesthood. You might recall that we pray this text from Philippians as the Entrance Antiphon to the Third Sunday of Advent or *Gaudete Sunday*, a Mass which commemorates the light of the pre-dawn breaking through the darkness of sin (it's also known for the priest wearing *rose* vestments at Mass instead of purple – *rose*, not pink... because *priests don't wear pink!!!*). The text reads,

> Rejoice in the Lord always. I shall say it again: rejoice! Your kindness should be known to all. The Lord is near. Have no anxiety at all, but in everything, by prayer and petition, with thanksgiving, make your requests known to God. Then the peace of God that surpasses all

understanding will guard your hearts and minds in Christ Jesus.[xxxi]

If we allow the Holy Spirit to shine through our hearts, then the words said to the priest at our future Masses serves as an acclamation and support of this God that we all want to rest within us. With God present in our lives, there is no worry or anxiety; there is no need or desire for fame or fortune. With God in our lives, all we seek is peace of heart, knowing that what God provides us may not always be what we want but will be overflowing more than we will ever need.

May we realize that this holy message is one that should be proclaimed more than once in the life of a priestly ministry. May this message of the Spirit's presence be a constant one in our hearts so that we may all see the good in those around us, around you and may the grace of the Lord Jesus Christ and the love of God be with you... and with your Spirit. This is our prayer.

9th Sunday in Ordinary Time (Dt 11: 18, 26-28, 32; Ps 31: 2-3a, 3b-4, 17-25; Rm 3: 21-25, 28; Mt 7: 21-27)

I adapted the following story from one of my homily resources...

Back in the Sixteenth Century, a woman once went to the sacrament of reconciliation to St. Philip Neri and confessed that she had been gossiping about others. As her penance, St. Philip instructed the woman to walk to the outskirts of the village in which she lived, taking a feather pillow with her along the way. The priest then instructed the woman to walk back home from the outskirts of town, releasing all the feathers from the pillow she carried with her. The woman followed the St. Philip's instructions and returned back to her church the following week to tell of her journey.

As St. Philip listened to the testimony of this woman, he praised her for her obedience and then gave the woman one last instruction. He said, "Now I want you to go back along the way and pick up all the feathers of the pillow that you have just released!" The woman was dumbfounded. The task was impossible. By now the wind had scattered many of those feathers miles away, out across the country.

St. Philip continued. "Now you see what has happened as a result of your gossiping. It is impossible to call the words back again, once you sent them on their way. Be very, very careful what you speak and especially what you gossip. It is generally impossible to repair that damage."[xxxii]

The reason I begin my homily with this particular story is not for your benefit but for mine. As is the case with most everyone in this room, one sin in my life of which I am very aware is the sin of gossip. I try to be aware when I am doing it and I certainly am aware during the times that it is being done to me. Whenever I focus on this particular sin in my life, I often turn to the Gospel of Luke, Chapter Six, verse

38, where I apply the following quotation to my life of sin as much as the author refers to this passage in the life of grace: "For the measure with which you measure will in return be measured out to you." When it comes to breaking the Eighth Commandment, I very much understand the moral of today's story, whether that moral applies to me or to someone else: *It is generally impossible to repair the damage of the sin of gossip.*

For the sake of this homily, I began to research in the Sacred Scriptures the various references that apply to the subject of gossip and came up with the following passages that our Lord has provided for us on this particular subject. The scriptures say:

> I will deal with them according to their conduct and according to their judgments I will judge them; thus they shall know that I am the LORD. (Ezekiel 7: 27)

> He who covers up a misdeed fosters friendship, but he who gossips about it separates friends. (Proverbs 17: 9)

> Like a crazed archer scattering firebrands and deadly arrows is the man who deceives his neighbor and then says, "I was only joking." For lack of wood, the fire dies out; and when there is no talebearer, strife subsides. What a bellows is to live coals, what wood is to fire, such is a contentious man in enkindling strife. (Proverbs 26: 18-20)

> We hear that some are conducting themselves

among you in a disorderly way, by not keeping busy but minding the business of others. Such people we instruct and urge in the Lord Jesus Christ to work quietly and to eat their own food. (2 Thessalonians 3: 11-12)

The tongue is a small member and yet has great pretensions. Consider how small a fire can set a huge forest ablaze. (James 3: 5).

In reflecting upon this weekend's readings, I was reflecting on the times in my life when I have "tossed my own feathers in the air" (in keeping with the theme of my homily). When I was ten years old, I used to remember attending Mass each week and trying to be respectful and attentive at the liturgy, only to find out that as soon as I left the church and went into the parking lot, I reverted back to the same sinful condition that I had before I walked into church. My mother used to chide me when I would act in this manner; at these times, my mother used to get very mad and say to me, "You just received communion, so start acting like you just did!"

Years later, I think that my mother's sentiment applies both to my current life and to this life of today's age. I think about in my life how many times I have tossed feathers from the church to the parking lot after the Mass has ended and the amount of times people have confessed at the sacrament of reconciliation about the manner in which they, too, have "tossed their own feathers" in the parking lot and beyond. Even for the short amount of time that the Blessed Sacrament digests within a faithful person (some fifteen minutes or so), the question arises within all of us whether our lives have actually become holier with the presence of Christ within us or whether that presence has been taken for granted.

The theme that scripture scholars attribute to this Sunday's readings very much parallels the sentiments of my mother's words from thirty years ago. Today's gospel from St. Matthew provides a fitting conclusion to Jesus' *Sermon on the Mount* passage, as Christ summarizes the basic theme of the Christian life that had preached to His disciples. For the faithful Christian, reciting the prayers and going through the motions of faith is certainly not enough. According to the scripture scholars of today's age, the Christian life is not just going through the motions but truly embracing and imitating the life of Christ. To them, when we *do not live* the Christian life, the result of such disobedience becomes greatly catastrophic for us.

When we embrace the scripture readings like those we hear today, we are challenged to enter the difficult side of the gospel message that just doesn't tell us about the rewards of the Christian life but the results of those who do not choose to live this way. I know that I do not like to hear about being challenged by others. As Moses laments in today's first reading, our life of faith is a blessing and a curse: a blessing for those who follow the life of God and a curse for those who do not. What bothers me as a person of faith is whether I have become akin to blowing feathers around the parking lot or anywhere else I roam. Where I struggle as a pastor is whether I can teach our flock to avoid the spreading of the feathers in their daily lives as well and adhering to the words of the Book of James, Chapter Six, where he calls the wise and learned person one who shows his life of faith through humility, wisdom and good works.

From this point forward, we begin the long haul of a series of twenty-six sets of readings that will carry us through the Season in Ordinary Time. As will be the case during the beginning of the summer months, we will see a drop off of Mass attendance here at the parish, sometimes due to vacations and out of town activities, other times through neglect of the Third Commandment. Those who do not attend Mass on a weekly basis will not have the opportunity to learn the type of Christian life that will permit them to enter heaven. The challenge in our lives is to remember that our God guides us just as much in the summer months as in the rest of the year and that God counts on us building a relationship with Him during this season as a prerequisite for us continuing this relationship in the kingdom of heaven.

This relationship must start at this Mass, which our Second Vatican Council described as "the source and summit" of our Christian life. This Mass strengthens us to live the Christian life, both in the parking lots, in our homes and everywhere we breathe. The question we must pose to ourselves is whether we wish to continue building this house on solid rock by building a relationship with God or whether we choose to build a house on sand that blows away at the first gust of wind.

Our *Prayer after Communion* very well summarizes the theme of today's homily: "Guide us with your Spirit that we may honor you not only with our lips but also with the lives we lead and so enter your kingdom." May we all learn to live the faith we profess and never toss feathers at the expense of others. This is our prayer.

10th Sunday in Ordinary Time (Hos 6: 3-6; Ps 50: 1-8, 12-13, 14-15; Rm 4: 18-25; Mt 9: 9-13)

This weekend, I had the honor and privilege of spending time with a Hispanic woman from Plano, Illinois named Maria. During the time that I celebrated Spanish Masses in Plano, I have encountered Maria numerous times at Mass, accompanied by her very tall daughter Socorro. We have seen each other in passing over the years, but like many parishioners I have met, I never really had the chance to talk to this woman at any length until I paid a call on her one day at her home.

I had not had the opportunity to see Maria for quite a long time, since my time in Plano has been sporadic for a good span of time. Out of the blue, Maria's daughter called me on the phone and told me that her mother had suffered great physical pain over the last year due to diabetes, which cost her both legs and a great deal of hope. Socorro told me that her mother was losing her strength and her faith and was in need of a pastoral visit from the parish.

I subsequently visited Maria and entered her room, encountering all the religious accoutrements that can be found often in a Spanish bedroom – statues, crucifixes, rosaries and the like. Maria was expecting me – she was sitting up at her bed and was overjoyed that a person of the cloth was willing to spend time with her. Little did she understand that the moment of faith that was encountered was more needed by me, not her. Sometimes the great people of faith seem shielded from noticing the presence of God that surrounds them; it often takes an outsider like myself to recognize that which has been present all along, reminding me that this same presence of God is surrounding me as well.

As I reflected on this weekend's readings, I started connecting the gospel message concerning Jesus' pastoral visit to the home of Matthew to my pastoral visit to Maria. My role (and the role of any minister who allows it) is to permit our Lord Jesus to speak through our souls so that it is the divine who is speaking to those who are infirm through the person of the minister. But the theme on which I would like to focus today is the recipient of the gift of faith. Matthew, like Maria, represents each and every one of us present in this Church today. Matthew is a sinner, a person who truly recognizes themselves as unworthy for this type of pastoral visit. Matthew, like Maria, is weak in body and mind and in search of a healing presence that cannot be found at the local drug store or hospital. As our Lord tells us in today's scriptures, when someone is in need of spiritual or physical assistance and when they turn to the Lord for help, it is as if the Lord descends upon them in such a special way that the sick person does not even recognize the holiness that has surrounded them.

Often in life, the outer world does not comprehend why the divine would spend so much time with people that the world would consider weak in comparison. The response that Jesus offers today echoes the themes of the words of today's first reading from Hosea and becomes the motto that every person in this room should follow, that we are all commanded to follow when we are commissioned at the end of Mass – we are called to take care of those who are most in need of God's presence. Jesus tells us in the scriptures today: "Those who are well do not need a physician, but the sick do... I have come to desire mercy, not sacrifice... I did not come to call the righteous but sinners."

I suspect this is the reason why many in third world and oppressed countries often pack their churches on a constant basis – those who are the most in need of God become the most faithful. In my experience of faith, some of those who are well provided may not see God as a necessity in life or may demand of God luxuries of which they may not deserve. When we attain positions of power or fortune, sometimes we apply that condition in areas where we are not necessarily as worthy. The fact is (and this is actually a positive statement), <u>none</u> of us are worthy of the presence of God; none of us have enough power or wealth to demand anything from our Lord. In a blink of an eye, the Lord can take away everything that we have been given. Yet, instead of depriving us of this great gift of faith, our Lord humbles Himself to serve us, to feed us, to visit us in our homes and to heal us of our spiritual illnesses.

As we return to the readings from Matthew's Gospel in this cycle of readings from Ordinary Time, we begin again with a story of both healing and service – to turn to God in need of His spiritual healing and to serve those, in God's name, who are less fortunate as us. May we call carry the banner of today's gospel as an inspiration to turn to our Lord and to turn to others in our Lord's name. Let us remember the themes of today's gospel: Healthy people do not need a doctor; sick people do... I have come to desire mercy, not sacrifice... I have not come for the righteous but for sinners. Let us come to the Lord as sinners and humbly bring this message of service to the Matthew's and Maria's of the world and all the people that we meet. This is our prayer.

11ᵗʰ Sunday in Ordinary Time (Ex 19: 2-6a; Ps 100: 1-2, 3, 5; Rm 5: 6-11; Mt 9: 36—10: 8)

I am a sinner. This testimony is the foundation for my homily and the foundation for my life if I am to understand today's gospel from Matthew and my own life in general. I know myself better than any human being in this room. I know what kind of person I am when I get behind the wheel of a car and am involved with afternoon traffic. I know that I am overly judgmental at times, that my first response to stress can often be that of anger and that I sometimes fly off the handle instead of stopping to reflect and pray over the crises that plague my life. I am a sinner and without God's help, I am mired in the yogurt of life from which I cannot escape.

Many times throughout my life, I have reflected on my sinful life and have turned to a book written by St. Augustine some 1500 years ago called *The Confessions*, a text that revealed this great saint as a sinner as well. The story of St. Augustine has been well documented, most notably by the saint himself. Prior to his conversion, Augustine led quite a hedonistic life. His father, his family, often turned away from the truth of God in order to focus on more selfish needs that occupied their time. It was through the prayer life of his mother, St. Monica and the assistance of the local bishop, St. Ambrose, that Augustine admitted his sinful nature and turned to the Lord in a great spirit of humility.

I have often preached in the past about the great role models of faith who accepted their sinful nature in order to empty themselves of this sin so that the Lord was able to fill their lives with a spirit of grace. I have preached about the sinful lives of Ss. Peter and Paul, both before and after their conversions. I have preached about St. Pope John Paul II's acknowledgement of his own sinful nature as well. I have reflected this week on the words from St. Paul's second letter to the Corinthians when he writes, "If I must boast, I will boast of the things that show my weakness."[xxxiii]

When I sit in the confessional and listen to the sins of people much holier and much more sacred than me, I enter into their lives and reflect on the type of life that these people wish to lead. When a holy person walks into a confessional and confesses that their prayer life is not as strong as they wish it to be, I begin to think how often I see this holy person engaged in prayer and that the so-called sin they profess pales in comparison to the much greater sins that are inflicted upon the world. I reflect on the holy person, thinking that their state with God is in such a place that, from their perspective, even a moment away from God seems like a cavern that separates the sacred from the profane.

I think to myself that if all of us in the world devoted ourselves to such a great life of prayer as the holy ones in our society have done, if we admit to our sinful condition and our great dependence on God as our saints have done, then what a better world we would have. With this great life of prayer, our eyes would be opened to drain ourselves of the petty desires of man and focus ourselves on the riches that God's grace has to offer.

Today's gospel focuses on the fact that all of us are sinners, that all of us are like sheep without a shepherd. We focus on the shepherd who leads us and guides us, who shows us the direction in which we all need to follow. In the Old Testament, our Lord guided us through the persons of Abraham and Isaac, of Moses and Aaron. In the New Testament, our Father reveals Himself through His Son, who reveals the face of God and allows us to see the presence of God, which gives us hope and direction.

When our eyes are focused on that direction through our prayer life, when our hearts are placed in the hands of our Lord so that we might be saved, then the places our Lord leads us are filled with His grace and spirit. The places that our Lord leads us may be filled with strife and grief, but in this life of prayer and God's presence, we are comforted with the words of strength our Lord gives us. In my prayer life, I especially turn to Psalm 23 and the fifth chapter of Matthew when I am in need of guidance from the shepherd who leads me: "Even though I walk in the valley of darkness, I shall fear no evil, for you are at my side with your rod and staff to give me courage."[xxxiv] "Blessed are they when they insult you and persecute you and utter every kind of evil falsely against you because of me. Rejoice and be glad, for your reward will be great in heaven."[xxxv]

Today's gospel calls us to be sheep and shepherds, to be led by the Lord in faith and then to share that faith with others. It is when we realize that without our Lord we are nothing but with our Lord that we have everything, it is then that we find our purpose in life and realize why we have been created in the first place. Let us find our perspective of faith in life, let us be led by it and let us share it with the people that we meet. This is our prayer.

12th Sunday in Ordinary Time (Jer 20: 10-13; Ps 69: 8-10, 14-17, 33-35; Rm 5: 12-15; Mt 10: 26-33)

This week it took two infirmed Marys to relieve me of my fear...

When I read about the theme of this weekend's scripture readings last Monday, I started to think about how fear plays a role in my life. The fact is that fear is an unavoidable condition that besets all of us in life and, in the life of faith, is a very necessary condition. In its negative connotation, Webster's dictionary defines fear as an apprehensive disposition; in its position connotation, the Catechism of the Church calls fear a disposition of reverential awe before God. The purpose of my homily today is to show how this fear and reverential awe of the Lord becomes the key component to alleviate the fear set upon us by the world in which we live.

Because of my human state in life, I constantly experience some type of negative fear, whether it is that of the unknown, of the future, or even of death itself. In our human world, many individuals will tell us that our success in life is predicated on the ability to conquer the negative fears that beset us. Others will tell us that this condition of negative fear can never be conquered and that our success in life is predicated on controlling it.

When I thought about the two Marys in my prayer life this week, I started reflecting on their ability to accept and embrace this type of negative fear for the sake of their salvation and my ability to follow their example by embracing this fear myself.

One Mary I encountered in 2001; the other Mary I encountered most recently. Both of them suffered from the sickness of multiple sclerosis, a condition that debilitates parts of the spinal cord and prohibits the brain to communicate with the spine, thus rendering parts of the body inoperative. For a good deal of time, both Marys have suffered from this condition and both were resigned to the fact that they would not be able to walk. Both were resigned to the fact that they were in need of another to assist them for the rest of their lives. In both cases, both Marys asked me if I would bring them communion so that they could receive the grace of God in their lives.

I knew that neither Mary acquired this condition through any fault of their own. When kids ask me why God would permit anyone to be sick or to die, I try to explain to them the context of what we read in our second reading today, that our human race *chose* to live in this world of sickness, violence and death when Adam and Eve at the forbidden fruit in the first chapter of Genesis. When Adam and Eve chose to disobey our Lord, they chose to live away from the life of perfection. Adam and Eve chose to live in the same imperfect world in which we now live. Because of this condition, the two Marys in this world both suffer this great injustice by acquiring a disease as a result of our Original Sin and choice to separate ourselves from God.

Whenever I visited these two Marys throughout these years, I often thought about how both of them suffered so unjustly and yet interacted with me with such a great smile on their respective faces. I was thinking to myself this week how, with the kind of life these two ladies had to endure, either of them could smile at all. I thought about the suffering each had to endure and whether they were angry with God, or afraid, or feeling a sense of desperation. Yet, because both had such great faith, they turned away from the one man who caused this life of fear and turned to the other who conquered the fear on the cross. Because of this new Adam, both Marys realized that the key to salvation was to realize that their faith in the new Adam of the New Testament cast away the fears of the old Adam from the Old Testament.

As I got to know each of the two ladies, what amazed me about both of them was their perpetually cheerful condition, considering that both suffered from multiple sclerosis for so long. I started to reflect to myself that both women resigned themselves to their woeful condition of bodily health, but were not deprived of their spiritual health. This is important to me; this is a condition that all of us must accept in order for us to enter the kingdom of heaven.

To assist my cause, I reflected on the life of another woman in this history of our faith who also suffered illnesses throughout her life and, like the two Marys, resigned herself to her bodily illness but never resigned her faith life in God. The woman on whom I reflected was St. Teresa of Avila (d. 1582), the great Carmelite mystic who lived during the time of St. John of the Cross. In 1970, Mother Church bestowed on her the title of "Doctor," a title given only to three women in the history of the faith (along with St. Catherine of Siena and St. Thérèse of Lisieux). This is the woman who wrote the great Spanish Taizé prayer that we often sing at the Spanish Masses throughout the world:

Nada te turbe, nada te espante
Quien a Dios tiene nada me falta
Nada te turbe, nada te espante
Sólo Dios basta.[xxxvi]

Let nothing upset you, let nothing startle you.
Where God is, I will not fail
For God alone is enough.

Similar to the lives of the two Marys I described, St. Teresa grew up in a life of ill health, which caused her great suffering throughout her time on earth. As she grew older, St. Teresa saw this illness not as a cause for suffering or fear, but rather as a condition of enlightenment. For Teresa, her suffering made her realize that her body was susceptible to the ways of the world, so she dedicated her soul to the ways of God through a life of contemplation. Through this cause, St. Teresa became such a great spiritual and mystical figure in the Church that the faithful of Spain from the 16th Century and beyond looked to her writings as a source of hope during their own lives of suffering.

Throughout her illnesses and pitfalls, St. Teresa kept a great sense of humor. A story is told on her behalf about a meeting she had with an important bishop of the time and the travels that took her to this meeting. As she reached the end of her journey to this encounter, St. Teresa dismounted her horse and, in the process, fell into a puddle of mud, upon which she raised her eyes to heaven and said, "If this is how you treat your friends, no wonder you have so few." This was St. Teresa's relationship with God, which was seen by the faithful as very approachable and loving.

In her writings, St. Teresa spoke of this negative fear as something important in her life, as a way to remind herself that without God, this negative fear would overcome her and her sickness would defeat her. This beautiful saint and doctor realized that the positive Fear of the Lord could overcome the negative fear of human nature and with the help of God, nothing would trouble her and nothing would harm her. From the 41st Chapter of her great writing called <u>The Way to Perfection</u>, St. Teresa summarizes very well the life of faith that she strived to lead. She writes,

> ...You see that, with these two things -- love and fear of God -- we can travel along this road in peace and quietness and not think at every step that we can see some pitfall and that we shall never reach our goal. Yet we cannot be sure of reaching it, so fear will always lead the way and then we shall not grow careless, for, as long as we live, we must

never feel completely safe or we shall be in great danger. That was our Teacher's meaning when at the end of this prayer He said these words to His Father, knowing how necessary they were: "But deliver us from evil. Amen."[xxxvii]

Through her constantly imploring of the Lord to lead her from evil, to lead her from fear, St. Teresa established the kind of foundation that I believe the two Marys achieved to live within their own lives. They all chose the right kind of fear to which they wished to adhere and found salvation in their lives as a result.

May we realize that the words of St. Teresa become a rallying cry for those of us in today's age to overcome the negative fears that constantly fall upon us. May we embrace this great poem of St. Teresa of Avila as the means to answer the Lord's call in today's gospel from St. Matthew – do not be afraid; you are worth more than sparrows or anything else in the world. With God, nothing will hurt you and nothing will startle you. For where God is, we cannot fail – *God is enough*. This is our prayer.

13th Sunday in Ordinary Time (2 Kgs 4: 8-11, 14-16a; Ps 89: 2-3, 16-17, 18-19; Rm 6: 3-4, 8-11; Mt 10: 37-42)

I loathe frijoles! If you do not know what frijoles are, they are a special food from Mexico often called "refried beans." I don't know how they are made (or more importantly, <u>why</u> they are made), but many Latin Americans love these legumes from the nether world and serve them as a side dish with most meals at home or in the restaurant.

This is not to say that I will not eat frijoles. Whenever I attend an event hosted by a Mexican family and their spicy Latin American cuisine, I very much enjoy the taste of taquitos, burritos, enchiladas and the like. At each visit, though, the Latin American families often load up my plate with rice and frijoles – that is part of the Mexican culture. When I receive this plate with the frijoles, I remember what my mother often taught me about hospitality – when someone takes the time to make something for you, you accept it graciously, even if the food is not of one's favorite variety. I have taken this teaching to heart, whenever serves me coffee or cold slaw or anything with the word "salad" in it – I eat it graciously and search quickly for another libation to wash down the taste.

By the way, I really do like beans, just not of the Mexican variety. The fact is, I *love* beans in most other forms, especially in the form of *baked beans*, coated in tomatoes and onions and bacon and even hot dogs. I am told that most kids will pass on the baked beans at a cookout, but if you are going to serve me chicken or beef at a summer outdoor event, I will probably dunk most grilled meats into baked beans like someone would dunk donuts into coffee.

I was honored some time ago when a family from my parish invited me to their house for a dinner; as a treat, they made a special plate of baked beans just for me. Mind you, no one else consumed this American staple but me. Mind you, the person who cooked this delicacy had never cooked baked beans before and had to call one of her relatives for any kind of recipe. (Mind you, I have been eating baked bean leftovers for the last three days.) That is a form of hospitality as well – doing something out of the ordinary as a symbol in order to show someone else how much you care for them.

The theme for our readings today is that of *hospitality*. All three readings, in one way or another, touch on this same theme. Our first reading from Second Kings focuses on a woman who invites a stranger into her home in order to serve him a meal. If we lived about 3000 years ago and read this story, or even if we read this story today, we might very well be shocked and appalled, since the idea of a married woman welcoming a strange man into her home would seem very unsettling to us. But the woman did just that for no other reason but that of faith – her devotion to God and her faith in God's will motivated her to serve a man who preached God's word to the faithful. Not only did she feed the prophet Elisha but she also housed him and took care of his daily needs when he passed through her town. Elisha's response to this woman's hospitality was a special intervention to the divine to gift this family with the gift of children.

In our second reading today, the gift of hospitality is seen through the sacrament of *baptism*. In this gift of water, we are born in to the life of God, who welcomes the faithful believer into a life of love that is not often seen from the outside. We are taught that water is a sign of life and death and so it is with the sacrament of baptism as well. As we are immersed into this water, we share in the death of our Lord on the cross and allow the Lord to suffer the pain of death for our sakes. As we rise from the water, we enter into the life of the Lord and the hospitality of faith which our Lord provides us. It is in this house of God that we are welcomed every moment of our lives. It is in this house of faith that our Lord resides in this tabernacle, that our Lord welcomes us around this altar, that our Lord forgives us our sins, heals us, sanctifies us and instructs us on our path to heaven. It is through this baptism that our Lord leads us from sin and, when we follow Him, constantly guides us to a place where we will always be fed and protected.

Finally, our gospel challenges us to follow the example of our Lord and become the host for those who enter into our lives. When we welcome the stranger, feed the hungry, clothe the naked, understand and follow the Corporal and Spiritual Works of Mercy that our Lord has given us, then we just don't listen to these words passively but go out and live out these words whenever we serve others. When we welcome others into this life of faith, we model the faith of the one who welcomes the believer into the life of the cross, the life of death and new life. When we live the Christian faith, the cup of cold water which Christ instructs us to offer to the little ones of faith becomes not just a drink but a symbol of the divine presence that leads us and guides us.

It is for that reason that I learn to accept frijoles in my life. The food that others serve me fuels my body for action (sometimes it fills my body *a little too much)* and in respect to my sense of taste, I may or may not like what others offer me. As a symbol, though, the food becomes a reflection of what our Lord does for us at the banquet table and every moment of our lives. May we learn to give thanks for the hospitality that we have received in life, both from the Lord and from the Lord's followers and may we model that service in the way we receive the people of the world into our lives. This is our prayer.

14th Sunday in Ordinary Time (Zech 9: 9-10; Ps 145: 1-2, 8-9, 10-11, 13-14; Rm 8: 9, 11-13; Mt 11: 25-30)

In reflecting about the life of faith, I have decided that all of us would be much better off to follow the life of a jackass than the life of a stallion. This sounds quite odd, but if you can get past the guttural notions that you might infer from this analogy, I would hope all of you might agree with this concept by the end of this homily.

Consider the life of the noble steed. Tall, sleek and with a finely combed mane, the horse appears as a dignified warrior-bearer during times of battle. We have seen grand fights on the movie screens depicting these battles of the cavalry, from *Lord of the Rings* and *Braveheart* to most movies starring Roy Rogers or John Wayne. Each year, we gaze into our television sets during the three races we call *The Triple Crown (The Kentucky Derby, The Preakness and The Belmont Stakes),* admiring those three-year-old equines coming out of the final turn, racing towards that finish line with great anticipation. We have horse shows, farm horses and pet horses that draw the admiration and love of those that encounter these beautiful four-legged animals.

Then there is the jackass. The name speaks for itself. Supposedly dumb, slow and ugly, the jackass comes to bear the symbol, for today's times, of something else that is not quite right for the world. I was thinking back in Quechultenango, Mexico (a mission city that the Chicago Archdiocese served for over a decade) where I witnessed the parish priest slowly and painfully ascending and descending the mountains each month on the back of a burro, serving the indigenous folk who were unable to attend Mass down in the city. I have preached on occasion about a five-hour journey I once took some ten years ago to Paracutín, Mexico while seated on a wooden saddle of an old, decrepit burro. After the long journey to and from the mountain on that pine, wooden seat, the results from such a journey made me walk in such a way that swore me off from ever riding a burro again.

The fact is, to ride a jackass is one of the most humbling experiences that could take place in one's life. To ride a burro is to realize one's lowly position in life – unlike the grand entrances of kings or dignitaries, the person who enters a town on a jackass symbolizes the life of a simple, unworldly sort.

It is this type of lifestyle that our Lord has impressed on us as the type that most reflects that of heaven. Throughout our scriptures, the symbol of the ass has been mentioned almost 100 times to parallel the life of humility that all of us have been challenged to live by our Lord. In the fourth chapter of the Book of Exodus, for example, Moses enters Egypt with his family on the back of an ass in order to confront the Pharaoh on behalf of the chosen people of God. In the 22nd Chapter of the Book of Numbers, God speaks to a pagan named Balaam, a person most unworthy of Yahweh's protection, through the mouth of a jackass, the meekest of all God's creatures.

In today's first reading from Zechariah, the prophet uses the symbol of the ass to represent the simplicity and peacefulness upon which the divine Messiah enters into this New Jerusalem, as opposed to the image of the grand stallion which symbolizes violence and war. The prophet writes, "See, your king shall come to you; a just savior is he, meek and riding on an ass, on a colt, the foal of an ass."[xxxviii] This same theme becomes evident in the 21st Chapter of St. Matthew's gospel. In Matthew's account of the Lord's final entry into Jerusalem, we once again focus on the mode of transportation on which Jesus approaches the town, the same humble means with which we have crossed paths in Exodus 4, Numbers 22 and almost 100 other times in the Old Testament. We encounter once again the same theme reiterated by the prophets numerous times in the Old Testament, that those who are meek shall inherit the earth.

One theme from today's readings is that God's word appears so powerfully that even the meekest of creatures are affected by the love of God. Moreover, a second theme for today's readings is that the meekest of God's creatures *are the most able* to recognize God's presence because the meekest of God's creatures symbolize the meekness of our Lord. The donkey represents the lifestyle most devoid of pride or arrogance that often consumes the life of those who turn to the trappings of the earthly life and are blinded from seeing the love of God. As modeled by our most humbled and peaceful Messiah on the cross, we are taught once again that the meek are symbolized by the Samaritans, the sinners, the sick, our own innocent children and, the world of non-sentient animals, by the poor and lowly jackasses that we often mock and disparage.

This is why the words of today's gospel become so powerful – the words of today's gospel remove us from the realm of pride so that we may enter the realm of humility and peace. Jesus tells us today,

> I give praise to you, Father, Lord of heaven and earth, for although you have hidden these things from the wise and the learned you have revealed them to little ones... Come to me, all you who labor and are burdened and I will give you rest. Take my yoke upon you and learn from me, for I am meek and humble of heart; and you will find rest for yourselves. For my yoke is easy and my burden light.[xxxix]

The gift that our Lord offers us today is the removal of the weight our earth has set upon us and has replaced this burden with the yoke of prayer and love, the yoke that removes poverty and violence and sin from our lives and opens our eyes to see the poverty and violence and sin of the world and then cleanse those ills of the world with the guidance of our Lord. We may choose to fight the world of man on the great steed of pride but we conquer the world while riding on the back of humility, by taking on an attitude of a child while wearing the yoke of Christ, a yoke of peace and love.

May we choose to engage this world wearing the yoke of Christ. May we solve the problems of the world in a spirit of prayer and peace. In the world of faith, may we all learn to value the life of a jackass. This is our prayer.

15th Sunday in Ordinary Time (Is 55: 10-11; Ps 65: 10, 11, 12-13, 14; Rm 8: 18-23; Mt 13: 1-23 or 13: 1-9)

A few years ago, I worked a couple of weeks in a mission parish in a Mexican pueblo called Quechultenango. In that village with rich soil and a beautiful year-round climate, I had the opportunity to visit many families in their homes, assisted with sacrament preparation and learned a great deal about life in a third world country. During my time there, I also ventured into the neighboring mountain territory, spending time with some of the farmers that grew crops on the sloped planes. On these occasions I felt like an honored guest, being treated like royalty in their homes with a bowl of pozole and a refresco while the families told me their stories.

One time while I was visiting these good people up in the mountains, I noticed that many Mexican farmers in the region did not grow crops as we do in this country. Here, in our very organized pattern in which we live, the rows of crops that we plant are straight and neat. We build irrigation ditches between the crops so the extra water will not ruin what we reap. We control the amount of weeds and bugs that surround the crops by flying airplanes over the fields and spraying insecticide on the plants. But in the mountains of Mexico, where none of these luxuries are to be found, the Mexican people can

Rev. Peter G. Jankowski

only take handfuls of seeds and scatter them wherever they can in the mountains, hoping that the seeds will take root and become fertile.

Our readings today show us that we all need to live in the mountains and become Mexican farmers in the world of faith. Our goal, as Christians, is to spread God's word to everyone we meet, regardless of who we meet. The gospel tells us that some people do not let the seed grow well in their lives, but that is not the point. The point is that the seed is always planted, God is always present and this offers us a great hope in our lives - even in the darkest of times, God is present to us. But we must do our part - we must plant the seeds of God in the things that we do. We must live God-like lives.

The problem with saying these things, by the way, is that we all know how much work it takes to spread God's word. We also know it is frustrating when we think some people do not understand what our Lord is trying to tell us. I have heard some parents say that they are frustrated because their kids do not see God in their lives. I have listened to good folks who have tried to do mission work and find it very difficult because many people do not listen to the word of God in their lives. Yet, once again, our role in life is to plant the seeds, to offer God to others. Our role is to accept God into our lives, to let the seed of God grow within us. When we can do our part in allowing this garden on earth to grow, then we take a step closer to seeing God in our lives. But we must plant the seed.

It is the Lord who asked us to help Him spread the message of God's saving word, as he planted them, throwing it everywhere, with abandon, without counting the cost, without taking precautions about where it falls, constantly preaching, constantly challenging, constantly letting it fall into the hearts of those who hurt, into the minds of those seeking the light, into the lives of those who sought the fullness of life.

It is a hard work and it takes lots of perseverance. There are so many people here in the faith who have been long at the work of spreading the seed of a gospel of life, of justice, of truth, of equality for the oppressed of this world. Today I want to highlight your work which, like what happened when the boy played with Paderwerski, is the wonderful result of the master working with the little people of the earth to create a new song of wonder and hope.

God's praise to you parents who persevere in planting God's seed of truth in your children! The difficulties are obvious and I'm sure they never seem to an end. Families are busier than ever. It's hard enough to get everyone around the table for one meal a day, let alone take time to open a bible, to spend time reflecting on God's word, to reflect together on the Sunday scriptures before or after Mass. It's not easy to compete with TV, soccer, band rehearsals and all the other activities that take kids here and there, anywhere but into serious reflection on their faith, God's word and the teachings of Catholicism. It's not easy to help youth understand why religious fidelity to Christ through regular worship is such a formative influence in their lives. Indeed, perseverance is a tough task and you deserve God's praise for sticking with it when it's more important than ever!

Today, I encourage all of you to go out to plant a garden today, the garden of prayers and service that produce God's love in this community. Every time we give another person hope with our prayer intentions or help out with someone who is needy, we offer hope and plant the garden. If we offer a smile and a kind word to the people that we meet, we offer hope and plant the garden. If we go home to our families and friends and do something together in God's name, we offer hope and plant a garden. Certainly the seeds are present in that diocese this weekend. Pray for each other, love each other and offer the hope of God to each other. In other words, plant a garden – God has provided the seeds! This is our prayer today.

16th Sunday in Ordinary Time (Wis 12: 13, 16-19; Ps 86: 5-6, 9-10, 15-16; Rm 8: 26-27; Mt 13: 24-43 or 13: 24-30)

I loathe broccoli... more than I loathe frijoles! (A 13th Sunday in Ordinary Time Reference) This is not to say I won't eat broccoli when it is served to me – I have gotten used to eating this horribly looking plant and I know that this particular vegetable is very good for your health. That said, I have a deep affinity to the words that the President George H.W. Bush once was quoted to say when he served as our president. President Bush once said famously, "I do not like broccoli. I haven't liked it since I was a little kid and my mother made me eat it. I'm President of the United States and I'm not going to eat any more broccoli." In this one way, my life as pastor parallels the first George Bush's dining habits as a president.

I pondered over President Bush's quote while praying over this weekend's scripture readings, connecting the philosophy of broccoli that President Bush and I both share with one specific instruction father gave to me about this vegetable some years ago. At that time, my father was travelling with his family for a month long vacation in Poland to visit the relatives. I remember quite well that I handled with care the many tasks that my father asked me to cover during his absence. During his time away, I checked his mail frequently, I fixed some odds and ends in the house, I kept the house clean and I made sure the lawn was mowed and kept manageable. During my father's month away, I accomplished every task that has been set before, save one: I refused to do any of the gardening in my father's backyard.

You see, the life of gardening and Father Pete Jankowski just do not go hand-in-hand. When I was younger and lived on the farm, my father used to assign me the "heavy lifting" tasks that I enjoyed doing in place of garden work. On the farm, I moved the heavy equipment and bags from "Point A" to "Point B"; my father assigned me to clean the sheep pen and make sure the animals were well-fed and watered.

The talents that I lacked the skills to do on the farm were the ability to perform the more delicate tasks. For instance, I could not garden. I could not tell the difference between the weed and the plant and often pulled out one when I was supposed to pull out the other. After a while, my father realized my shortcomings in the vegetable patch and relegated me to the tasks of life that I was able to accomplish.

Because of this, I told my father how apprehensive I was in messing with his garden as an adult, fearing the same shortcomings that befell me some years ago. I did the best I could, but I had no clue on how to maintain the garden. I knew at least how to pick the red tomatoes, which seemed easy enough to do – you pick the red ones, not the green ones. But even I could notice that the vegetables were starting to rot and I panicked.

Acquiring the Wisdom of Solomon about two weeks after I really needed it, I visited one of my father's neighbors for some assistance with my problem. The neighbor showed me the difference between an under ripe, ripe and overripe vegetable. He showed me that some of the cabbages in the garden were starting to mold and that if I did not pick the others, the others would suffer the same fate. The only good news from this whole mess (at least good news for me, that is) was that the all the broccoli has gone to seed and was no longer edible – *boo hoo*. Please know how distraught I felt over not being able to eat that disgusting vegetable for the remainder of the summer; George Bush would have been proud of me.

When I read today's gospel from the 13th Chapter of Matthew, I found some comfort in the words that were spoken with my garden experience from some years ago – let the weeds grow with the wheat and on the last day the weeds and the wheat will be separated. I like that idea – leave the delicate work until the end and relegate my faith life to the tasks of heavy lifting. The problem for me, though, is that this reading kind of contradicts the text from the early portion of Matthew's Gospel, Chapter 13, the early portion of the text that we read from last week's gospel. In that text, our Lord lectures us that the soil upon which the farmer lays his seed must be rich and fertile in order for the seed to take root. Last week, I preached how the land on which we work, the faith in which we live, must be well cultivated and cared for in order that the seed find a suitable growing place, a place that is ready and receptive for the rain and grace that our Lord showers upon us each moment in our lives. So which is it – should we prepare our land well and make our faith lives receptive to the grace of God or should we allow the weeds and sin and evils of the world grow around us and let God take care of separating both at the end?

Some biblical scholars contend that the portion of Matthew's Gospel that we read today may very well have been inspired by the faithful that lived in the time after Christ's death and were trying to reconcile their lives of faith with the evils of the world that surrounded them. This view is supported by the words of the first reading from Wisdom, which states that a loving and forgiving God will pardon the sins of the faithful believer, will cleanse them of the wrongs they may have done and will remove them from these stains of sin to live in a symbolic garden without the weeds of temptation.

In reflecting on these passages from the last two weeks, I can only conclude that we must accept the fact that we live in what I call a "both and" society. We must accept the fact that the faith life we keep must be well-prepared to receive the graces of God

<u>and</u> that the world of sin is probably growing all around us as we speak. We must accept the fact that the only ground that we are able to control fully is that of our own faith lives. We have the ability to prepare our faith lives to receive God, even though the people around us may reject the faith and may very well tempt us to do the same.

We also must accept the fact that we can only do so much for the sake of others in the world, that we are challenged by our Lord to try and make this world a safe place for others, but we do not have the ability to force others to make their faith lives as rich as ours strives to be. Many times in the confessional, the faithful have lamented how their good works seem in vain, how they try to instill the faith on the members of their families, only to see the members of their families turn away from that faith in order to walk their own path.

To this, we must be resigned to knowing that the consequences of a free will and original sin are the consequences of people choosing whether to follow good or evil. As a human race, we chose to understand this difference the hard way in the Garden of Eden and as a result, our eyes have become open to the full force of evil in our lives. Each one of us has the choice to turn away from sin and believe in the gospel. But we are not robots – we cannot force others to follow our path. Each person in this world must make the choice to make their faith lives rich to receive the Word of God or to allow their faith lives to grow barren or hard or full of thorns or weeds. In the end, each one of us will be accountable for our individual actions – it is God who will remove the wheat from the weeds, the faithful from the sinners.

The bottom line is that we are limited by the number of ministries we can accomplish in the world; there is only so much we can do. If we are aware of the talents that God has provided for us, then we also know what tasks God has assigned to us to live in this garden of faith. If we believe in this one, holy, Catholic and apostolic Church, our hope is that others in our society might take care of the broccoli plants that we may not have time to cover or that we avoid altogether. Our hope is that God will provide for the other missions in life while we focus on the ministries that God has assigned us to do.

I am certain that some in the community may write letters to the bishop about my sinful attitude concerning one of God's vegetables (please spell my name correctly if you do). May God teach us to eat our vegetables, tend to our own gardens and to pray that we can work together to take care of all of God's land and those faithful who dwell upon it. This is our prayer.

17th Sunday in Ordinary Time (1 Kgs 3: 5, 7-12; Ps 119: 57-72, 76-77, 127-28, 129-30; Rm 8: 28-30; Mt 13: 44-52 or 13: 44-46)

One of my friends who once worked for the diocese paid a visit to our parish some time back, joining us for a special Mass intended for her mother. Mary and I have known each other for a good number of years and her family has a dear place in my heart.

Some years back, her mother was enduring the

same type of suffering that many families have the misfortune to experience with their loved ones. As with many of these families, I walked through this difficult journey with Mary's family which led to her mother's untimely death, her funeral and beyond. Mary intended a few Masses here at the parish for the sake of her mother, which gives me an opportunity to reacquaint myself with both her and her family. Often we have the chance after these Masses to bread break (or more specifically tortilla chips) and share stories together.

As this story played out, with her mother's passing Mary was reaching a crossroads in her own life. With her father living alone on their farm, Mary had to make that painstaking decision as to whether she would leave her job to spend time with her father or to continue working while constantly worrying about her father's well-being. For those of us who have reached a certain age, the prospects of deciding how to care for our elderly parents, or how our younger children choose to care for us, turns into one of the most challenging decisions we have to make on this earth. Especially when you love someone dearly, making such a grueling resolution concerning the care of our parents causes great stress both for the parents and their children as well.

As Mary was grappling over this challenge, I was reminiscing about a similar time when I, too, had to make life-altering decisions for the sake of my own father. Back in 1988, I was just finishing up my graduate studies at the Catholic University in Washington, D.C. in pursuit of a master's degree in philosophy. As I came to the end of my studies, the Diocese of Rockford told me they wanted me to study as an upper graduate seminarian in Louvain, Belgium during the next stage of my seminary formation.

As I was given this news, it dawned on me that if I accepted Belgium as my future, I would be living out of the country for four years, come back for my priesthood ordination and then serve the Church as a priest for the rest of my life. If I had chosen this path, I would never know what it would be like to date, to rent an apartment or to take care of some of the necessities of my life on my own as those in the secular world often do. At the time, my vocation director told me that decisions in life are better served if I truly knew what paths were available to me. He encouraged me to take time off my studies if I was not sure of my vocational path.

On May 12, 1988, the path for my life was chosen for me. Everything changed. On this date, my mother horribly died in an automobile accident in my hometown of Sandwich, Illinois.

With this sudden passing, everything in our family came undone. My father could not handle the prospect of living alone while my two brothers and my sister were struggling with this great sudden loss. The person to whom I turned in my life journey was no longer present to me physically to rest upon in this transitional period of my life. In short, my mother was the emotional center of my family and without her as the glue, our family was falling apart.

In my heart, the Lord was telling me at that time to leave the seminary for a period of time so that I could take care of my father. Instead of pursuing my vocational call to the priesthood, I decided to move back home. For four years, my father and I got to know each other all over again and our relationship changed. Whereas I felt my relationship up until that point was paralleling Harry Chapin's "Cats in the Cradle," all of the sudden two ships passing in the night were able to stop and spend time together in the same waters.

Still, my dad was struggling with this great loss and needed guidance on how to pick up the pieces. To that end, we spent a great deal of time together, eating many dinners that I would prepare (he thought I used too many onions and garlic in my cooking preparations but what did he know???). We sat and watched many movies together on the VHS. What once was lost was now found again – the Prodigal Son had returned home and reacquainted himself with his father.

In an attempt to turn his life around, my father visited to a seventy-year-old priest from the neighboring town named Fr. Boniface, one of the most kindred spirits you could find on life's journey. During their time together, Fr. Boniface assured my father that his life <u>did</u> have meaning after his wife's death and that he still had something to contribute to society.

So my father got his act together. He began to date, he found a woman he loved, he got married and at the time of this preaching has been married for over twenty-one years with a son that will turn twenty-one in December.

As my father rekindled his own life, I also rekindled mine and chose to return back to the seminary. As a seminarian now for the Diocese of Joliet, I attended the University of St. Mary of the

Lake in September of 1992, was ordained four years later.

I learned that the only reason I have succeeded as a priest (if I have succeeded at all) is with the help of God and because of the treasure that has presented me in the form of my family. When you find a treasure that is so important in your life, you sell all you have and devote your entire energy to embracing that treasure. You realize that when you devote your entire treasure to that which is most important in your life, guided by the Lord, then no fame, fortune or popularity will ever equal the joy and grace that fills your heart when you share an anniversary moment with a couple in love or a graduation service with someone who labored for the sake of a good education. When you love in God's name you find that no greater satisfaction can be embraced in this world than the presence of God in the hearts of those you serve and love.

So in Mary's case, she has come to find out that the presence of her father, at this time of her life, has become her greatest treasure and gift from the Lord. In Mary's case, she may not attain the type of wealth with her father that she could earn in the working world but she also knows that when the time comes for her father to leave this earth, she will have the satisfaction of knowing that time has not been lost with her father. With this quality time, Mary will not encounter the "Cats in the Cradle" moment with her dad and, as a result, she has now found a peace in her heart that can never be taken away.

A great coda to this story. When her mother was alive, Mary's parents bought an old 1927 Ford Model-T pickup truck from a neighbor who found the truck too difficult to maintain. Mary used to tell me that her parents used to drive that truck around the country every Sunday as part of their Holy Day together. How many seniors have reminisced with me how Sundays used to be family days, with the family attending Mass together, taking drives in the country together and then sharing a meal at the dinner table together, at a time when conversation and family-building time was not invaded by television or hand-held devices?

Mary told me that this last month, someone from the area was able to repair the 1927 Ford Model-T pickup truck so that he could take Mary's father for a drive in the country as once was done in years past. Mary lamented that she could not put a rocking chair in the back of the truck to drive with them but she did not want to be called "Granny Clampett" by the neighbors if she did (I think you have to be over forty to get that reference).

I wish to conclude today's homily as I would for the funerals that I celebrate as a priest. If we truly love someone in their life, then we commit ourselves to sharing that love with those around us. Maybe today would be a good day to recognize the treasures sitting within our own community and in our own homes. Maybe we can take a moment today to tell those in our families how much we love them and spend time with them so that the words of love we speak are not empty words. Whether we take a drive in a Model-T Ford pickup truck or cook dinner with too many onions and garlic, the time we spend with our treasure in life is treasured time.

May we share God's love with the treasures that we meet. May we realize that everyone that we meet is a treasure because every person is created and loved by God and should be loved by us as well. This is our prayer.

18th Sunday in Ordinary Time (Is 55: 1-3; Ps 145: 8-9, 15-16, 17-18; Rm 8: 35, 37-39; Mt 14: 13-21)

Some time back, I met a couple from the Joliet area with whom I have continued to build a wonderful friendship. Don & Sue were/are parishioners of a neighboring Church where I serve. In his working days, Don ran a flourishing business as a CPA and Sue always assisting Don with the workload. As I came to find out, Don & Sue established their business by word of mouth and over the five decades that they served the area, their presence at the finer eateries in Joliet has drawn them to many business associates and life-long friendships.

Now I am a morning person who was taught in life about the value of spending time with parishioners over the breakfast menu at your friendly local establishments. It was through this practice that I began this friendship with Don & Sue. One morning a few months ago, I was joining Don & Sue for our sunrise encounter when next to their table I spotted two empty chairs sitting next to the place we customarily sit. I figured that a table was once placed between these two chairs that sat in the middle of the restaurant; at the time I entered the restaurant, the table was nowhere to be found.

As I passed by the chairs, a group of men who also frequented the restaurant were kidding me about the chairs which had no home. "Hey Father," they said to me, "since the chairs aren't doing anything in the middle of the restaurant, why don't you hear confessions for us?" As a joke, I sat on one of the chairs and invited the men to come and have their confessions heard. To my surprise, someone from the table took me up on the offer and asked me to hear their confession.

Now I am not endorsing restaurant confessions as part of my ministry. However, I have noticed that as a Catholic priest, I have been called upon to invest in my vocations at the most unexpected times. You never know as a priest when your services might be utilized – I famously remember a couple recognizing me in Disneyworld as I was taking my ten-year-old brother on vacation (thank goodness the family knew that the ten-year-old was my brother!). I spoke to the person who took up my invitation of the empty chair and asked the person sincerely if they needed to talk at that moment, which they did. I asked her if it was alright to meet in a quieter place in the restaurant, where later in the morning I heard their confession.

On another occasion – same restaurant – I was leaving breakfast when someone was waiting for my outside for the same request. The person suggested that we speak inside their 4x4 Dodge Ram Pickup Truck, which I happily did. I did not seek out the confession but the confession in the Dodge Ram Pickup Truck sought out me, I guess. When I asked why they did not just come to church to have their confession heard by the priest on call; they responded that the line was too long in the confessional and knew that I had frequented the restaurant!

Because we are devoting this weekend to St. John Vianney at St. Patrick's, I present these stories to you because the gospel message today talks about a physical feeding that satisfied the body which parallels the more important message of our God who wishes to feed our soul with His forgiveness and grace. To the former we are always seeking assistance; to the latter, we often seek out God only when we are in true need of God and not before. As a society in general that takes a more utilitarian and hedonistic approach to life, God does not often find a place to rest, although God creates all and has the desire to fill grace in all.

Concerning the charism of St. John Mary Vianney, I often desire somewhat incapably to embrace the gift of forgiveness that flowed through his soul. Fr. Oliver Günst Horn, a French priest who is spending the weekend with us, told me that the village that St. John Vianney served is occupied only by about a thousand residents today – the village is not very big. Yet, even though the village was small, the people kept venturing into this little village because Fr. John Vianney kept hearing confessions and saving souls. Because St. John Vianney provided a type of care that the faithful not only desired but returned back to so often, I realized in my own faith life that the only way to recapture that desire was to offer the sacrament in the same type of manner.

As I shared with you a few months ago, this sacrament is a blessing for all of us, as it offers a type of forgiveness that we do not often receive from our family and friends, a type of forgiveness that wipes away the past and begins life anew without any type of judgment. When I serve as the priest confessor, I find that the sacrament does even more for me – it reminds me how I, the sinner, encounter so many holy souls that strive to live a life clean of sin, inspiring me to become a better person as well to those whom I serve.

As I reflected on this theme of forgiveness in preparation of what we are about to do, I came across a dialogue that our Holy Father sought out with a group of priests and bishops from the Italian city of Caserta. In the midst of this dialogue, a priest from the diocese posed the following question to Pope Francis: "What suggestion can you give us for a ministry that, without devaluing popular piety, can re-launch the primacy of the Gospel?" As part of his answer, the Holy Father covered the same subject matter that I offer you in today's homily. Pope Francis responded,

> Popular piety is active, it is a sense of faith—says Paul VI—deep, which only the simple and the humble are able to have. This is great! In sanctuaries, for example, we see miracles! Every July 27, I would go to the Saint Pantaleo Sanctuary in Buenos Aires and I would listen to confessions in the morning. I would return renewed from that experience, I would return shamed by the holiness I would find in simple people, sinners but holy, because they would tell of their sins and recount how they lived, the problem of their son or their daughter or of this or the other and how they would visit the sick. A sense of the Gospel shone through. In sanctuaries, you find these things. The confessionals of sanctuaries are a place of renewal for us priests and bishops; they are a course in

spiritual renewal because of this contact with popular piety. The faithful, when they come to confess, they tell you their miseries. But you see behind those miseries the grace of God that guides them to this moment. This contact with the people of God who pray, a pilgrim people, who manifest their faith in this form of piety, helps us a lot in our priestly life.[xl]

This is the beauty of ministry – as a child teaches the parent about life, so the sheep do the same for the shepherd. This grace of God is a mutual giving, as we grow with each other in this path to salvation. Only when we invest in this life of the faith by forgiving and being forgiven do we understand the import of what Christ did for bodily hungry in today's gospel and the spiritual hunger that constantly exists in our lives as well. We are called to never allow this seat of forgiveness to go empty, for the seat constantly is presented to us as a gift that our Lord wishes to offer us in love.

For every moment when the chair is taken, a soul is being saved and our work as evangelist is geared towards the salvation of souls. Let us learn about this gift of forgiveness not by abandoning it but by taking the Lord up on His offer of this sacrament. This is our prayer.

19th Sunday in Ordinary Time (1 Kgs 19: 9a, 11-13a; Ps 85: 9ab-10, 11-12, 13-14; Rm 9: 1-5; Mt 14: 22-33)

Does anyone get frustrated with "Salt & Pepper Fights" in life? I certainly do – I have had to experience them most of my cognitive days on earth. You turn on a television, the reception is horrible and what usually results is a screen full of static that covers over any attempt at watching anything on TV.

When I looked up the phrase "static noise" in an online dictionary, I came upon two definitions that very well describe the torturous sounds of the radio and pictures on a television. According to Collins English Online Dictionary, the phrase "static noise" is defined as "random hissing or crackling or a speckled picture caused by the interference of electrical disturbances in the reception of radio or television transmissions" or more simply, "electric sparks or crackling produced by friction." I call static "Salt & Pepper Fights" as an abbreviation.

This subject has been in my thoughts lately because my car radio all of a sudden is engaged in this "Salt & Pepper Fight" drama whenever I try to listen to music or anything else while I am driving. Maybe something in the City of Joliet is interfering with my reception; more likely, maybe it's time to get a new car (which my salary isn't going to allow in this life). For me, there is nothing more annoying than filling the car with the noise of static which, to my, is equivalent to someone scratching their nails on a chalkboard.

Really, Salt & Pepper Fights are my father's fault. My father is a fanatic of classical music.

Unfortunately, only one radio station in Chicago plays the type of music that my father enjoyed, a station whose signal was much weaker than its more popular counterparts. Thus, whenever we drove any distances in my father's car, I would be tortured listening to a 30% blend of music I didn't like and a 70% blend of electric sparks or crackling produced by friction.

My childhood leisure time was always filled with static. Unlike today's age of high definition cable or satellite television, I lived out in Sandwich, IL in the middle of the country with a cheap antenna connected to my TV. In those formative days, the only television stations that would reach our home were Channels 7, 9 and 11, sometimes Channel 5 & 32 and *never* Channel 2. The only thing I could watch with decent reception was "Bozo's Circus" and Cubs' Baseball Games and sometimes even these shows were interrupted by Salt & Pepper Fights. This pretty much summarizes why I am the tortured soul that I am.

I was reminded of these horrendous thoughts one time during a Mass at Stateville Prison. To give context to what I do at Stateville, our Mass is celebrated on the second floor of the gymnasium building; during recreation time, some of the inmates are down below playing basketball and getting their exercise. Up above one group of inmates are engaged in a bible study program with a minister from the Salvation Army while other inmates are celebrating Mass with me.

So at Stateville Prison that fateful Thursday, I couldn't even think very well because my words were getting drowned out by what seemed like a swarm of basketballs pounding around the room we were using. The inmates below were not doing anything wrong but the sound was deafening. The noise of those orange globes was extremely distracting. In the world of concentration, I was losing the battle against the Salt & Pepper Fights on the basketball court and I had a difficult time keeping focused on what I was doing.

Here, after a long prelude to the readings for today, is the point of this metaphor – how many times have Salt & Pepper Fights in the world of faith distracted us into building a relationship with God? We live in a society today where our options for work and leisure are so diverse and plentiful that we often sacrifice our relationship with God to pursue something infinitely less important? You know what I mean – you say that God is important in your life and you really do want to pray but when you try to pray you become distracted by the static of life, those things that look very desirable but have no substance? If you were given the choice between the best cooked vegetable in the world and your favorite snack, which would you choose? Only those who say that the best cooked vegetable *is* their favorite snack is the one who finds true satisfaction in life.

Look at today's scriptures as our example. In our first reading, how is Elijah able to hear the Lord? In the static of life represented by the wind, the earthquake and the fire we are incapable of encountering the Lord because our lives become cluttered and distracted. This is what Satan wants from our lives – Satan wants us to be distracted because the more we pay attention to the static of life the less we desire to be with the Lord. But when we remove the clutter of life to hear the whisper, when nothing else matters in life but the whisper, then we truly and deeply fall into a love with God that makes everything else insignificant and our lives become singularly devoted to the work of the Lord. The moral of this story, as told by the scripture scholars, is that for those of faith, our Lord speaks to us and saves us not with great fanfare but in a whisper. Should this not be the manner in which we serve each other in the name of the Lord?

In our psalm reading for today, the people lament over the losses that they have endured in life and how often has that happened to us? How often have we lost that which is most precious to us, our faith lives themselves, because our relationship with God has disappeared in the night? The response from the Psalm of Lament is one of hope – listen to God, put your trust in God and the Lord will deliver you from the darkness in which our lives have languished.

Then there is the famous gospel reading about Jesus walking on water, which is the focal point of today's readings. Look at the disposition of Jesus in today's gospel versus the disposition of the apostles and, metaphorically, us as well. The boat in which the disciples sit, in Latin, is called *the nave,* which is the same term we use for the place in which the faithful sit at Mass to reflect on the word and to share in a meal. In this boat, we are protected and separated from the world of static so that our minds can be cleared to encounter the Lord without distraction.

In today's gospel, while the Lord prays quietly while keeping the boat in sight, the apostles in the boat become afraid because the distractions outside of the boat have preoccupied their thoughts. Instead of finding comfort inside the boat knowing that while they are inside they are kept safe, they are more consumed with the situation outside the boat, which even the Lord is able to overcome through the image of Him walking upon the water. When St. Peter, called by the Lord to keep focused on the Lord when invited to walk towards Him upon the water, loses focus for an instant and becomes consumed by the water over which he has the ability to overcome.

What gives me hope in our parish, what gives me hope inside this particular boat, is that the faith life of this community is evolving to realize that all the distractions that occur outside the boat are irrelevant and pale to the faith that we find within. The more we focus on prayer and God's presence in our lives, the more that we understand our own true purpose in life and the power that this nave affords us in the life of faith. This is why I feel so blessed when those in our community spend time in prayer during our all day adoration and confession times, our prayer opportunities such as the Círculo de Oración or our Legion of Mary or even the social and social justice events that bring purpose to the time we spent together.

This entire homily was inspired by the words of Pope Francis and his talk with about 50,000 German altar servers who spoke with him in Rome on August 6th, words that can apply as much to adults as they do German children. One of the altar servers offered a compelling question to which the Holy Father responded, one that reminded me about the static that afflicts my own life at times. I would like to end my homily by sharing this question and answer with you today...[xli]

Question: Holy Father, I really like being an altar boy. But sometimes it is not so easy to be one. Some Sundays I'd rather have a good night's sleep; other times I have other commitments, such as playing sports or playing a musical instrument. Whatever my decision, I find myself to have a little remorse. Some of my friend do not understand why I want to be an altar boy, tease me or resent me, maybe because this commitment allows me no time for anything else. Can you give me some advice on how I should handle this situation?

Answer: I understand your difficulty to *reconcile the commitment to ministering with your various activities*, which are necessary to your personal and intellectual growth. We all need to organize and plan balanced things ... but you are the Germans and this will be good! Our life is made of time and time is a gift from God, so you must engage him in good deeds and fruitful. Perhaps many young people lose too many hours in futile things: we probably spend too much time *chatting* on the internet or mobile phones or watching the "soap operas," which are the products of technological progress. These things should simplify and improve the quality of life and yet these same things sometimes divert attention from that which is really important. Among the many things to do in the *routine* of our daily lives, one priority should be to remember our Creator that allows us to live, who loves us and who accompanies us on our journey.

Just because God created us in His image, we have also received from Him the great gift that is *freedom*. If you have not exercised this freedom well, however, freedom can lead us away from God and can make us lose the dignity with which He has covered. This requires living within the guidelines and rules of this freedom, both in society and in the Church, to help us to do the will of God, thus living according to our dignity as human beings and children of God. When that freedom is not shaped by the Gospel, freedom can turn into slavery: slavery of sin. Our first parents, Adam and Eve used this freedom to turn away from God's will and subsequently fell into sin; that is the wrong use of freedom!

Dear boys and girls, do not misuse your freedom! Do not lose the great dignity as children of God that has been given! If you follow Jesus and His Gospel, your freedom will blossom like a plant in flower and bring abundant good fruit! You will find the authentic joy, because He wants us to be men and women who are perfectly happy and fulfilled. Only by adhering to the will of God, we can do good and be the light of the world and salt of the earth![xlii] [Francis, "Meeting with Altar Boys from Germany," (translated by Peter Jankowski... badly)]

Let us take the words of the Holy Father to heart as we choose to engage in this life freedom as protected and framed by the gospel message. This is our prayer.

20th Sunday in Ordinary Time (Is 56: 1, 6-7; Ps 67: 2-3, 5, 6-8; Rm 11: 13-15, 29-32; Mt 15: 21-28)

I have a dirty dog living in my house! I am speaking, of course, about a literal "dirty dog," my sixty-pound basset hound named "Rusty Joe Troublemaker."

I give you this information as an introduction because Rusty, frankly, is in a great need of a bath. Every time he encounters "bath day," Rusty fears who he considers his mortal enemy who drives to the parish in a van marked with the words, "Paz Pampered Pets." The nice lady that exits the van is as pleasant as can be but Rusty has a sixth sense whenever that van approaches the house. I can tell when Deb the Paz Pampered Lady is anywhere near the rectory because Rusty, all of a sudden, is nowhere to be found. In these cases, I usually can find the pooch curled up in a ball underneath one of our office desks, so fearful he is of soap and water. My problem with a basset, of course, is that as soon as he is clean, he runs outside to find the smelliest mess he can find to return himself back to his previous condition (which is kind of the way our human race in general sometimes acts as well).

If I told you that my basset hound was a dirty dog, you would probably would agree with me and maybe laugh, knowing what kind of dog Rusty happens to be. If I happen to call a human being, *any* human being, a dirty dog, then this is a completely different story.

Rev. Peter G. Jankowski

To be called a "dirty dog" in our human history would be a grave insult in any age. Maybe among friends who enjoy "locker room" talk or ten year olds from the movie "A Christmas Story," this language may seem right at home. In civilized society, though, calling a person a dirty dog is a seriously pejorative term.

Not that this term hasn't been used in the bible in this particular sense, though. The bible makes over sixty references to dogs in the scripture, most of them in a negative way. In both books of Samuel, the term "dog" is seen as a type of human debasement that lowers the human being to a sub-human level. In both books of Kings, the fate of King Ahab's kin (including his wife Jezebel) is lowered to a feast for the dogs, which pretty much is their comeuppance for the type of life that King Ahab and his wife chose to lead. In the gospel of Luke, the poor man Lazarus lived such a pitiful life that even dogs licked on his sores. In today's gospel, Jesus refers to this Canaanite woman as a dog as well because she was a person not of the same faith as those in Jesus' inner circle.

What was Jesus' intention in our gospel reading for today? Was Jesus truly using language more fitting for a locker room than for the Son of God? Was possibly that the author of this gospel was implementing a literary device to use a play of words to demonstrate the great faith of the woman in question? These questions are still debated by our bible scholars of today but what is *not* debated is the faith that an outsider held in a gospel primarily written for Jewish Christians.

This point is key, especially for those who choose to follow the Christian path. How many times have we encountered those "outsiders" in the scriptures who have demonstrated this type of remarkable faith that they are afforded this grace even more so in some respects than those that often go through the motions of the faith but do not embrace the message of God in the soul?

There are so many examples of religious people different from us that we have discussed repeatedly who have great faith according to their customs and ways of life! In the scriptures we have encountered Syrians, Syro-Phoenicians, Samaritans and all the rest grouped together with the term "Gentile," many of whom demonstrating the type of faith that all of us are called or even desire to live. St. Paul goes out of his way, as presented in our second reading today, to dedicate his life to drawing the life of the outsiders in, to dedicate himself ministering to the Gentile folks with such passion and love that today we give him the title, "The Apostle to the Gentiles." In our gospel today, a Canaanite woman whose life those of the faith would casually disregard modeled a type of faith that all of us should aspire to live.

What is the message from today's readings? Could it possibly be that whenever we label someone as a "dog" or "infidel" because they do not share a common faith or heritage with us that we open ourselves to be labeled in the same way? How often do we abandon the same faith that we claim to follow? If we use this criterion to label other people, then at times we have to label ourselves as dogs as well! To be people of faith, we must recognize ourselves as sinners in need of redemption.

For this reason and more, we are obligated out of love to realize that every person we encounter is a person created by God, embedded with God's Spirit that can be seen every time we extend a caring hand and kind word in their direction. This love and care cannot and must not be directed exclusively to our family and friends – Jesus warned us of this in His Sermon on the Mount. In addition to what we normally do, our Lord shows us the potential to do more, to extend ourselves beyond our comfort zones to love and serve those we do not know. Until we are able to call each and every person in the world our brother and sister, even if they do not afford us the same courtesy, we are far away from embracing the Lord eternally in heaven.

May we learn to break down the barriers that separate us. May the words we use build us up instead of break us down. In the world of faith, there are no dirty dogs, only souls in need of finding God's path, created in God's image through His likeness. Let us help them on this path as we offer a fraternal hand to the people that we meet. This is our prayer.

21st Sunday in Ordinary Time (Is 22: 19-23; Ps 138: 1-2a, 2b-3, 6-8; Rm 11: 33-36; Mt 16: 13-20)

A few years ago, I came upon a free ticket to travel anywhere that United Airline flew. I had so many choices and so many places I wanted to visit. In the end, though, I felt most comfortable going back to where I call "home" – I decided to use my ticket to travel to Vatican City and spend a week on retreat at what I call Mother Church's "Home Base."

Towards this cause, I found a cheap hotel near the Vatican where I could spend my week. The hotel room was no larger than a college dorm but the hotel was located next to this wonderful Italian restaurant with a veal chop bone that could have starred in a "Flintstones" cartoon. As I checked into my room, I determined the schedule of my self-guided retreat at the Vatican – I would visit a Vatican basilica by day and dine on a Flintstone-sized veal chop at night.

I decided to take this journey on retreat because there is a storied history behind the four basilicas that are under the Vatican's control. These four places of worship are the preeminent basilicas in the world; if you go to visit all four and pray for the pope's intention, there are indulgences involved with those visits. The basilicas also have special significance – thanks to Pope Pius XI, the Catholic Church was able to preserve these basilicas when the Italian Dictator Benito Mussolini coveted all the land in Italy possessed by the Catholic Church. Thus, in 1929 Pope Pius signed what we call "The Lateran Treaty" with Mussolini, a treaty which allowed Italy to take possession of all Vatican lands and for the Vatican to take possession of the four basilicas in Rome and the 120 acres surrounding St. Peter's, creating an independent city-state which serves as the smallest country in the world.

So each day on this retreat, I spent time at one of the four Vatican Basilicas. On Monday, I went to visit the Basilica of St. John Lateran. Prior to the enemy forces invading the Vatican lands in the early fourteenth century, the popes lived at the Basilica of St. John Lateran, making their official pronouncements on a special chair or *Cathedra* that adorned the basilica's sanctuary. For seventy years, the popes lived in Avignon, France, protected by the country's government and establishing the Church's seat of power for that period of time.

The next day, I visited St. Peter's Basilica, the location where the popes returned after their time in France, a basilica where the popes have lived ever since. Especially in the 15th & 16th Centuries, the beauty of St. Peter's was enhanced through Renaissance art and baroque statues that fill the worship space with beautiful images that point towards God's presence. I remember standing in line for confession, praying the rosary for the souls of the parishes I served and being blessed that the priest hearing my confession was from Ireland, sharing with me the story of his faith life. It was a great experience.

The third day, I spend my morning at St. Mary Major's basilica, which is walking distance from the basilica of St. John Lateran. Pope Francis once stated that he did not travel a great deal in Rome before his pontificate but he made time every trip to stop at St. Mary Major's basilica, so important was the place in his heart for the Blessed Mother. You might remember that very shortly after his papal election, the Holy Father made a special trip to this basilica for a time of prayer that was very important to him and extremely inspirational for us.

The fourth day was my favorite – I happen to like the spirit of God found in the basilica of St. Paul Outside the Walls of Rome. Located outside the boundaries of the city (hence the name), St. Paul's is run by the Benedictine order and has been preserved for many years. The most impressive feature of the basilica, for me, is that the perimeter of the upper walls contains pictures of the 266 popes that have headed the Church, from St. Peter to Pope Francis (whose mosaic portrait was added in 2013).

When I gaze upon the images of these popes in St. Paul's Basilica, I very much reflected on the histories of these 266 men who have sat on the Chair of St. Peter. Each of these men have a story about the faith to tell – sometimes the stories of these men have been sacred ones; sometimes the stories have not been as sacred. Eighty-Three of these popes have been canonized in the Church, Popes John XXIII and John Paul II being the most recent [prior to their election, the last pope to be canonized was Pius X (1903-1914) and before him was Pius V (1566-1572)].

The oldest of the popes that was elected was Pope Adrian I, who was 80 years old at the time of his election. The youngest of the popes was Benedict IX, who purportedly was 12 years old at the time of his installation (though some claim that he was actually 20 years old). According to tradition, St. Pope Peter was the longest serving pope; St. Pope John Paul II served in the papacy about twenty-seven years, the fifth longest tenure as a Holy Father. The shortest reign for a pope was Stephen II, who lasted in the papacy just one day.

In our history of the popes, Pope Benedict IX was elected pope three times during a schismatic time in the Church when three men claimed to be pope at the same time during what historians often call "The Great Western Schism of the Church." St. Pope Celestine V (to whom Pope Francis has declared this year in his honor) was elected to the papacy in 1294 but vacated his position shortly after his election. The only other pope to leave the papacy voluntarily was Pope Benedict XVI in 2013.

Even over the last 100 or so years, the popes who have held the keys to the kingdom have done so with great weight on their shoulders. Pope Leo XIII (1878-1903) was the champion of the labor movement, the herald of what we call labor unions today. St. Pope Pius X (1903-1914) began the start of the 20th Century liturgical movement by proposing that the language of the liturgy should match the language that each country spoke. Poor Pope Benedict XV (1914-1922) had to endure the weight of World War I and his futile efforts to bring peace among warring nations. After a so-called peace was established among the European nations, Pope Pius XI (1922-1939) struggled valiantly against the Italian dictator Benito Mussolini in order to preserve Vatican territory, as stated at the beginning of my homily.

In the history of the last hundred years, my soul grieves at the manner in which Pope Pius XII (1939-1958) had to struggle throughout his papacy. Fearing great retribution by Hitler and the Nazi Party for defending the life of both Jew and Christian, Pope Pius wrote a scathing attack on Hitler during the Christmas of 1941, an attack which promoted the New York Times to write, "The voice of Pius XII is a lonely voice in the silence and darkness enveloping Europe this Christmas."

Remarkably some twenty years later, a Nazi sympathizer wrote a play called "The Deputy," reducing the role of Pius XII to that of "Hitler's Pope." For a Holy Father that helped forge thousands upon thousands of baptismal certificates for his Jewish brethren and then hiding them in churches and basilicas from the Axis forces, the work of a few put the evil blood in the water of hope that Pius XII offered the Church during a most horrendous time of the faith. To this day, this poor man's soiled reputation had caused great scandal to both him and a society who raised him up as a beacon of light some seventy years ago.

Following the pontificate of Pope Pius XII, the cardinals chose to elect "Good St. Pope John XXIII" (1958-1963) who served as pope for five years. Pope Francis likes to say that Pope John liked to see everything, turn a blind eye to most and change little, but the little thing he changed was called Vatican II, a council which very much changed the manner in which we prayed and viewed one another, not as people separated by language and tradition but as brothers and sisters united in God's spirit.

After St. Pope John's death, Pope Paul VI (1963-1978) continued the work of his predecessor and continued the work of the Second Vatican Council. At that council, the bishops throughout the world redefined how liturgy and social action in the Church took place as well as setting guidelines towards the way we taught, lived and trained future leaders of the Church. The work of these two popes was of such great importance that the next pope chose to take both of their names, "John" and "Paul" as a testimony to the work of Vatican II that would continue in the life of Pope John Paul I (1978). Unfortunately, this Holy Father served in this capacity for only a month. It was then that the cardinals elected the first non-Italian pope in 450 years, St. Pope John Paul II. During his pontificate, the Code of Canon Law was revised, the new Catechism of the Catholic Church was promulgated, communism was defeated in Europe and the pope visited more countries in twenty-seven years and had canonized more saints than almost all the rest of the popes combined had done before him.

As I reflected on the lives of all these popes at the Basilica of St. Paul outside the walls, I often realize that the world of the papacy is one of great responsibility and of great weight.

Yet, above all else, one quality of the papacy stands head and shoulders above the rest, as our current Holy Father shared with the Jesuit journalist reported by Antonio Spadaro, S.J., editor in chief of *La Civiltà Cattolica*, the Italian Jesuit journal (and reprinted in the US by *America Magazine*). In this article, Pope Francis mentions that as a human being on his own human journey, Jorge Bergoglio serves as nothing more than a sinner who seeks redemption just like the rest of us. As quoted of Pope Francis, "(Who is Jorge Mario Bergoglio?) I do not know what might be the most fitting description.... I am a sinner. This is the most accurate definition. It is not a figure of speech, a literary genre. I am a sinner."

what the pope says makes sense. Look at today's gospel as an example. Matthew's gospel is the only one of the three parallel gospels (namely Matthew, Mark and Luke) where Jesus responds to Peter's call of faith by presenting him these "keys to the kingdom," this metaphorical gift which opens the spiritual doors that separate the human world from the divine.

What is Peter's response to this gift in the additional text which corresponds to this gospel reading? Immediately after this declaration, Jesus tells the apostles of His upcoming suffering and death, at which St. Peter, the first pope of the Church, in his first act as pope commits a sin by remonstrating our Lord and putting God in his so-called place. what is the response of our Lord to the patronizing Peter – He tells him, "Get behind me, Satan! You are an obstacle to me. You are thinking not as God does, but as human beings do." (Mt 16: 23)

Every single Holy Father has the same faults as the rest of us – we are all sinners on this road to salvation. Yet, these 266 Holy Fathers have also been given a great trust by the Lord and a great calling to continue the work of faith passed to them from previous generations as we are called to do the same in our local churches, our families, our communities and our respective dioceses. The pope is in Italy and we are here – the pope has been called by God to do one type of work and we are called to do another. All of these roles are important and all of them make up the body of Christ.

As a priest who stood under these images of the 266 popes and reflected on the ministry each one served, I prayed that I would be able to serve in a small way with the same conviction and Spirit that was afforded these men by God. I prayed that I might be worthy of my role as they prayed they be worthy of theirs, knowing full well that the faithful Christian realizes that none of us are worthy of this gift but constantly strive to become worthy of this gift.

In whatever the calling of God be for us, may we all embrace that call, recognize our weaknesses and share this presence of God with the people that we meet in whatever ministry God has presented to us. This is our prayer.

22nd Sunday in Ordinary Time (Jer 20: 7-9; Ps 63: 2, 3-4, 5-6, 8-9; Rm 12: 1-2; Mt 16: 21-27)

A few years ago, I was giving a homily at one of my previous parishes and I thought I had my homily down cold! I was thinking how every cylinder was on that week and that the words I spoke really captured the gospel message and connected with the experience of the human condition. When I delivered that homily, I watched the faces of the people in the congregation and saw how the message resonated with them. As each moment passed, I was feeling the Spirit moving deeply within the community. At the end of Mass, as I was talking to the congregation and was hearing a rather positive response concerning the homily, an elderly parishioner came forward and put my entire homily in perspective.

"Father," she said, "I really wanted to pay attention to your homily but I was distracted when I noticed that you were wearing two different colored shoes during the Mass..."

I remembered another time shortly after I was ordained. I was working at a parish with a small church building and there was a Mass where 200 or so people were standing outside of the church because there was no seating left inside. Being a creative and ambitious priest, I decided to celebrate an impromptu service in the basement of the church and invited those outside to join me. The service was great! People were singing, volunteers came forward to read and help with communion and by the end of service, I really felt great in that I could help a group of people be involved in something very spiritual.

HOWEVER, the pastor was furious at me when the service was over, not because I celebrated the service but because I forgot one essential element that Sunday. Think about it – what is the one thing at Sunday service of which the pastor thinks about a lot but the associate pastor rarely does? The answer: *the collection!* The associate pastor forgot to take up a collection! (Needless to say, the pastor gave me a crash course entitled, "Parish Business Management 101!")

It seems to me that if we had to, we could make a video of all my bloopers, mistakes and such both on and off the altar and pay off the parish debt with the proceeds. I suppose that we could do that with anyone here. I think that if we had to talk about one common denominator that all of us have, it would be the fact that we are all human, that we are all sinners. Only two people who have lived on earth escaped the hazards of sin: the Blessed Mother and our Lord Jesus. As for the rest of us, our lives are filled with bloopers and faux pas that dog us all.

I guess there are a lot of things about which I could preach concerning our readings today. I could talk about Jeremiah's anger against the Lord concerning the destruction of the Jerusalem Temple in 587 B.C. I could talk about our need to prepare for the Judgment Day and what will happen if we are not prepared. But what struck me most this week in the readings concerned Peter's fallibility. Whether one is a pope or a priest, whether one is an ordained minister or a baptized Christian, we all are fallible at one point or another in our personal lives. They key is to understand that we are weak, to admit that we are weak and then to turn to the Lord to overcome that which brings us down.

Of all the saints in our Church Martyrology, the three that play the most influence in my faith life are the three who were brought down by sin and who allowed God to help them climb back out. Those three saints are Peter, Paul and Augustine. St. Peter was the one who often put his foot in his mouth. At the transfiguration, he blurted out lousy ideas when he should have been in awe of the vision he had seen. At Gethsemane on the night before Jesus' death, he fell asleep in the garden. He denied Jesus' divinity three times and in today's gospel, he patronized the Lord and tried to put Him in His place, at which time the Lord rebuked Peter and put him in his. Yet, despite his sins, Peter was given the preeminent place by the Lord in heading the Church.

Then there was *Saulos Paulos,* a man who devoted the early years of his life to persecuting Christians. Here was a man who stood off at a distance watching a group of people stone to death one of the first deacons of the Church, a man named Stephen. Here was a man at whose feet the persecutors threw their cloaks in honor of his presence. Of all the people that God could have chosen to preach and write down the ways of God, God chose the sinner to do his work. Because of this choice, Paul changed his life in 36 AD, he brought the message of God throughout regions that were never permitted to follow Christ and was rightly titled the "Apostle to the Gentiles" for his tireless work.

Finally, there is St. Augustine. As the story tells us, St. Augustine abandoned the faith of his mother, St. Monica, early in his life, turning to a life of a great sinner. In the process, Augustine lived in a concubine, had children out of wedlock and lived a pretty scandalous life. Yet, despite his grave shortcomings, God strengthened the resolve of his mother and holy people like the bishop St. Ambrose to pull Augustine back into the faith. As a result, Augustine became the great theologian of the Western Church and one of the most prolific authors within Christendom.

My fear is that if any of these three lived today, they probably would have been dragged through the mud and crucified, possibly literally, more likely journalistically. We have a habit of chastising others for their sins while trying to shield our own. The motto of television news is, "If it bleeds, it leads"; the motto of the newspapers is "if digging dirt sells one more paper, then dig the dirt." The motto of society is to tear another down to build another up, a motto that politicians have turned into a science and the gossips of our world turn into a recreational activity. The fact is, we all are sinners on the road to salvation and the only way to overcome our sins is to admit our sinfulness and offer it up in prayer.

As a response, the Church pleads to all of us to live the life of reconciliation. As God has forgiven us, so we must learn to forgive others.

This is all that God asks of us in today's gospel: to recognize that we are sinners and to forgive others who have sinned. When we place ourselves above the Lord, we suffer the sin of pride and become damned. When we humbly come before the Lord to confess our sins and to love others, then we get the gospel message. Let us humbly come to this table and recognize our faults. Let us forgive the faults of others. Let us share this meal as a common fellowship of sinners. This is our prayer.

23rd Sunday in Ordinary Time (Ez 33: 7-9; Ps 95: 1-2, 6-7b, 7c-9; Rm 13: 8-10; Mt 18: 15-20)

"Love means never having to say I'm sorry." This was the tag line to a film made in 1974 called "Love Story," which won an Academy Award for Best Song. The first time I heard that phrase, I had to ask myself if I was missing something – is this truly a sentiment that couples believe or even people of faith? I found my answer on the Internet Movie Database (IMDB.com). When the principal actors in this movie were asked what they thought about this iconic line, they all responded in the same way, namely that the line of dialogue was a bunch of nonsense. I guess what sounds good for motion pictures is not always good for real life.

For the next two weeks, our readings focus on these words. Our focus is on loving others instead of hating others. Our focus is on reconciliation. Unfortunately, this seems to be just as difficult a word for people to understand as "I am sorry." When we forgive people, we no longer have something that gives us power over that other person. As St. Paul says, we no longer have a debt of another. Yet, in this society, when we have a hatred or an anger against someone, we have power over them. That power takes over and consumes us. When we loathe each other, we no longer hold God close in our hearts, but instead replace God with an anger that spreads in our bodies like a cancer.

What we need in this world is more love, more God. What we need in this world is to turn our lives to God and ask God for his loving presence. St. Paul tells us today that love is the fulfillment of the law and the law is Christ. But to understand the law we need to love. If we loathe each other, if we do not seek forgiveness, we can never hold Christ because we can never find Him. Love binds, but hatred and anger breaks us apart.

As a priest, I have seen this love in others. I have also seen this loathe. As a priest, I hear confessions on Wednesday and Saturday afternoons and during the week. I see how damaging and dangerous this hatred is in people's lives. I see how people are looking for God in their respective journeys, how at times they lose their path to God and then how they come to confession to rekindle a relationship once lost. Is it not a beautiful thing to say the words "I'm sorry" and then be guaranteed to be loved and forgiven for what we have done? When we acknowledge our sinfulness, something miraculous happens. In the confessional, God comes down and touches these people with such a loving presence that those on the receiving end need no longer fear; if they allow it, the penitent is provided a gift of healing to cleanse them of pain and hatred in their lives. For the penitent sinner, the gift to start fresh begins all over again.

Yet, I fear that many people do not like to go to reconciliation because they do not want to tell anyone their deepest fears or their deepest sins. Sometimes it seems like we want to hold on to our sin more than we want to hold on to love. When sin becomes more important than love, then we lose our fight with life. Whenever we come to this sacrament of reconciliation, we personally touch God, we personally receive His forgiveness. What God gives us in this sacrament makes us feel more alive than sin can ever give us.

The saint we often associate with this type of forgiveness is St. Maria Goretti, whose day of martyrdom we commemorate each year on July 6th. Living with her widowed mother in the area of Le Ferriere di Conca, near modern Latina and Nettuno in Lazio, Italy at the early years of the 20th century, an eleven-year-old Maria helped her mother with the daily chores on the farm on which she was raised. During those formative years, a young neighbor of 18 named Alexander attempted to force himself upon Maria to the resistance of this 20th Century saint. Maria refused these advances, declaring that she would rather be killed than submit herself to Alexander's evil intentions and the sins of impurity. As a result, Alexander killed Maria, which both inflamed the hearts of the faithful of Italy and ennobled the hearts to honor an eleven-year-old girl who had the strength of will greater than many of us in these pews today. As Maria was dying, she forgave Alexander for his sins, which inspired her legacy of the time even more.

Sentenced to jail for thirty years, Alexander took a great deal of time to learn about the heinous crime he committed but with the aid of a local bishop and the support of his family, Alexander finally admitted to his sin, asked forgiveness from Maria's family and devoted the rest of his life to that of a Capuchin brother in the life of service to the Lord.

As for Maria, her forgiveness of Alexander on her deathbed became an inspiration to the faithful of those in Italy who had come across her story. As her faith inspired the masses, her cause was brought forth to the leaders of the Church and in 1950, Pope Pius XII officially canonized Maria Goretti as one of our recognized saints in the Catholic Church.

The prayer that we often associate with Maria Goretti very much falls in line with the teachings of our scripture readings today. For us to be forgiven of our faults, we must first forgive the sins of others. Ezekiel speaks of this forgiveness, as does our Lord in the gospel today. For those who live the Christian life, much will be given; for those who do not, for much will they have to answer. Here is the prayer that we dedicate to St. Maria Goretti:

Saint Maria Goretti,
strengthened by God's grace,
you did not hesitate, even at the age of twelve,
to sacrifice life itself to defend your virginal purity.
Look graciously on the unhappy human race
that has strayed far from the path of eternal salvation.
Teach us all and especially our youth,
the courage and promptness
that will help us avoid anything
that could offend Jesus.

Obtain for me a great horror of sin,
so that I may live a holy life on earth
and win eternal glory in heaven. Amen.[xliii]

In this Church, Christ works through His ministers to offer people forgiveness. During these readings over the last three weeks, we have heard Christ proclaim twice, "whatever you declare bound on earth shall be held bound in heaven and whatever you declare loosed on earth shall be loosed in heaven." I encourage all of you to come forward this month and as often as possible, so that through the priest, God and the Church may offer you the gift of forgiveness. If you have not gone to confession over the last years, I invite you to come back to God, come back to his love.

I encourage you to make a commitment to reconcile with your Church and God. Make a commitment to be cleansed by the Lord of all hopefulness. Let us learn today that the words which bring us together and make us strong simple and necessary: I am sorry, I forgive you and I love you. This is our prayer.

24th Sunday in Ordinary Time (Sir 27: 30—28: 7; Ps 103: 1-2, 3-4, 9-10, 11-12; Rm 14: 7-9; Mt 18: 21-35)

In order to appreciate today's readings, you must like fried chips or some type of junk food. Have you ever seen a kid with a bag of chips in their hand? They guard that bag of junk food better than the secret service guard the President of the United

States. After consuming this fried goodness with gusto, your average junk food kid inevitably peeks into the bottom of the bag to make sure he or she has cleaned out every last corner. You see, a bag of chips may be the most important thing in that kid's life, until ten minutes later when something else becomes more important.

Now imagine this kid eating that bag of chips and another kid walks by. This second kid passes by that smell of that artery-clogging carb, stops and asks the first kid if he would share what is in the bag. The first kid begins to panic. Should he give up the seemingly almighty fried chip? Sometimes the answer may be yes and sometimes the answer may be no. In the world of junk food, life can be a very difficult one.

By the way, this story happens every day, but not only with chips. This story can apply to when a person holds on very tightly to a friendship or even the love of God. Each of us possesses the greatest gift that God can give us – *our lives*. So the question is, do we share the gift with others, do we offer our love to others, or do we just hold onto that love without ever giving it away?

Our gospel for today tells us of a king who had power over all of his servants and the ability to take away their lives with a single word. The king meets one of his servants who owes him a great deal of money. In the gospel, the amount of money this servant owes is more than we would ever make in our entire life. The servant knows he cannot pay the king back, so he asks for mercy. The king could have held on to this power, but instead gives it away and the servant goes free.

In this story, the king is God and we are the servants. Every day, God gives us this gift of life, gives us more than we possibly deserve or need. Most importantly, God gives us an example- as He does for us, so we must do for others. God gives love in the gospel, He offers His love through this Mass and He offers His love any time we come together in His name.

So how do we respond? Do we offer the same love to others that God offers us or do we follow the example of the servant in today's gospel and abuse this gift? Do we hold on to the bag of chips or do we share them with others? Our readings tell us today that God will treat us the same way that we treat others, but in a way greater than we can ever know. If we love others, God will love us more than we possibly can know. When we insult others or hurt others, we are punished in a way worse than we can ever know. When we hurt others, we separate ourselves from God and while the rest of the world lives in God's loving embrace, we live in pain and fear. All we need to do is ask God for His love. All we need to do is ask God for His reconciliation. All we need to do is offer others the same love that God offers us. When we offer that love, God gives us more mercy than we deserve.

As St. Paul tells us today, let us live and die in the Lord. Let us bring all our joys and pains to this altar and ask God for His love. Let us remember to offer forgiveness to others and seek forgiveness ourselves, through the sacrament of reconciliation and this sacrifice of the Mass. Let us always remember that our King is the most loving, just and compassionate person in our lives... and pass the chips! This is our prayer.

25th Sunday in Ordinary Time (Is 55: 6-9; Ps 145: 2-3, 8-9, 17-18; Phil 1: 20c-24, 27a; Mt 20: 1-16a)

Here is the truth: in many ways, life is not fair. If life were fair, the people who worked hard would get paid well and there are a lot of people who work hard in this world who are not paid well. We all see people in this world who work really hard in school or in their families and they are not treated in the best of ways. Sometimes in this system of jurisprudence, people are convicted for crimes that they did not commit and yet they spend many years in jail for that crime. If we all think about it, there are many other things in life that are not fair, from the way oil companies raise gas prices to some ways the government spends our tax money. No, there life is not fair in many ways.

But here is a second truth, a more important truth: be glad God is just and not fair. If God were fair, then He would treat each of us in exactly the same way that we sin against others. Even if we repented in a fair system, we would still have to pay for our crimes. If we counted every sin that we have committed in this world and placed them before a fair God, He would have no choice but to punish us in the same way that we punished others.

So instead of being fair, God is just. Whenever we come to God in reconciliation, He forgives us of our sins. Even if we come to God at the end of the day and most of the work in our life is done, God will give us His forgiveness. If we truly give our life to God and pray for others, God will reward us in ways better than we can know.

We encounter this message in today's gospel. Here is a God who offers all of His love to any person that comes forward in the same way a farmer pays every worker the same amount of pay, even if the worker shows up the last hour of the day. Think about this- we have a great hope in a God who will accept us and our sins, but we have to come forward, ask God for His mercy and forgiveness and live the life of a Christian. When we come forward, God gives us a love that is not fair, but just. We can never earn the amount of love God gives us, but He gives it to us anyway.

For the last few weeks, the readings from Matthew have talked about ways to draw ourselves closer to God, through the sacraments of reconciliation and the Eucharist. In general, many people tell me they do not like reconciliation because they have to confess their sins. Over the last few weeks, Matthew tells us that if we want this wonderful gift of love, we must come forward and offer our lives to God, we must place ourselves and our sins in front of God and then we must go out and offer that love to others. Have we done this? Do we go to reconciliation? Do we leave this building and lead a Christian life, or does Christianity end as soon as Mass is over? I leave this building and ask these questions to myself as I live the life of a priest: Do I open my heart completely to God so that I may become a person through whom God can work? Each of us must ask ourselves the same question, the questions that our readings present us today: Do we seek the Lord? Is Christ exalted through me? Let us listen to the words of the Psalm today, which offer us great comfort in life: "The Lord is just in all His ways and holy in all His works. The Lord is near to all who call upon Him, to all who call upon Him in truth."

Yes, we should be thankful that God is just and not fair. If you have ever felt this love in your life, you know what I am talking about. Seek this love, offer it to others and let us share it together as we celebrate our sacred meal. This is our prayer.

26th Sunday in Ordinary Time (Ez 18: 25-28; Ps 25: 4-5, 6-7, 8-9; Phil 2: 1-11 or 2: 1-5; Mt 21: 28-32)

I am calling today's homily the theology of the "Blah Blah Blah," the "Yada Yada Yada" and the "Mwa Mwa Mwa...!!!" I have always been intrigued in the last reference, as it is the unintelligible sound that adults make in *Peanuts* television cartoons. I always wondered how the producers made the adults sound the way they did in the TV cartoons, so looked up the answer on the internet (Check out the Peanuts Animation and Video Page at http://fivecentsplease.org/tv/peanuts-tv.html - thank you Scott McGuire!) and I came up with the answer:

> According to Leonardo Moran of Bill Melendez Productions, "Composer John Scott Trotter directed his trombonist (to use a plunger mute and) to 'enunciate' the teacher's dialog as though it were a trombone riff. Trotter... would read the teacher's line, e.g., 'Linus, where's your

homework?' then direct the trombonist to repeat Trotter's inflection through his instrument."[xliv]

I was inspired by this reference during a recent liturgy I celebrated at the parish. No offense to my congregation, but I notice that sometimes a couple of the faithful are not giving their undivided attention to the teachings that the celebrant is offering during the liturgy – at times I might be guilty of the same sin! I also have noticed that I am much more aware of the attention deficit when I am on the receiving end of it instead of the giving end.

I liken this "Liturgical A.D.D." (Attention Deficit Disorder) or to what police officers often call "distracted driving" when folks are on the road. Instead of focusing on the road ahead of us and around us, we often are engaged in calming down children, putting on makeup, using hand held electronic devices or a myriad of other activities in the place of the one that is the most important. How many times do we recite "The Pledge of Allegiance" or sing "The National Anthem" and not even pay attention to the intended sentiments that fill the words we speak? How many times do our parents or bosses ask us to do something and we respond "Ya Ya Ya" when in reality all we hear coming out of their mouths is "Blah Blah Blah," "Yada Yada Yada" or "Mwa Mwa Mwa?" How many times can we actually recall? the gospel reading for the day or the homily attached to the gospel even one hour after the Mass has ended?

In my reflection of today's gospel, I see today's reading from Matthew 21 as a type of "sequel" from the fifth chapter of Matthew's gospel with a proclamation our Lord offered during His sermon on the Mount. In the course of His sermon from Chapter Five, Jesus challenges us with these words: Let your 'Yes' mean 'Yes,' and your 'No' mean 'No.' Anything more is from the evil one,[xlv]

In that light, I started pondering the manner in which we speak and the manner in which we listen and came across paragraph #2153 from The Catechism of the Catholic Church, which states the following: "Jesus teaches that every oath involves a reference to God and that God's presence and His truth must be honored in all speech. Discretion in calling upon God is allied with a respectful awareness of His presence, which all our assertions either witness to or mock."

Although this paragraph from The Catechism specifically refers to the second of the Ten Commandments, "Do not use the Lord God's name in vain," I reflected on the bigger picture this week concerning the manner we act like God, we listen like God and we speak like God. As I celebrated three services in one day that conferred a baptism, a First Communion and a wedding at the parish, I was reflecting on the seriousness that we take these promises that we make prior to receiving each of these special gifts from our Lord.

Think about a baptism. Prior to the reception of the sacrament, the priest instructs the parents concerning their responsibilities of raising their baptized children in a Christian household. Following the instruction, the parents are asked to make baptismal promises on behalf of their children, promises that the parents assure the celebrant that they will instill in their children during their upbringing. Think about how many times other parents, or even us ourselves, uphold their teachings through our actions and our words.

Think about First Communion. As a condition for receiving the sacrament, we instruct the students that they are required by the law of love (and the first precept of the Church, as well as the Third Commandment), they are supposed to attend Mass every Sunday and that skipping Mass on Sunday is considered a grave sin only because they are missing out on building and growing into a relationship with God in the most intimate way the Lord has provided for us.

Think about the Sacrament of Marriage. In a positive light, I was thinking about a woman from this parish whose husband became crippled through a debilitating illness. For years, this man was chair-ridden, unable to walk or even do the basic things of life that we often take for granted. Now here you have this woman who made a promise on the day of her marriage to take this man as her husband, "for better or for worse, for richer or for poorer, in sickness and in health, all the days of her life." In a society where getting a divorce can be a readily available as a prize inside a Captain Crunch box of cereal, this woman stayed by her husband's side not because of a martyr's complex but because she *loved* the man. For this woman, she took those vows seriously. In this example, I am not trying to make a blanket statement about annulments and divorce, as each marriage case is unique. What I am asking is how seriously do couples enter into a marriage – do they truly understand who they are marrying and the commitment they are making?

"Say 'yes' when you mean 'yes' and 'no' when you mean 'no.'" If you say "no" to your Father, reflect on the reason why you have done so, considering that the Father has called us for a specific reason and that we need to show respect to our Father. To take an oath is tough stuff – to answer "yes" to the call of God can be fraught with danger. No one said it would be easy to be a Catholic priest or a Catholic parent. But we are the ambassadors for God in our respective households and our children are God's most precious gift. If we set the example, then the kids are more likely to follow it; if we abandon the example, then the kids will follow that example as well, for our actions are a microcosm for our true views of life and our actions speak louder than our words.

As we prepare to recite our "oath" of the Nicene Creed, may we truly understand what we are saying when we pray the "Creed" or the "Our Father." May we always be cognizant that our actions today condition us in the manner which we treat others and demonstrate to others the type of Christian life we choose to live. Let us live our lives well, let the words we speak and the gentle listening that we offer have actual meaning and model those of the one who gave us life. May our words and actions not be worthy of a "blah blah blah" – may they be worthy of God's love in heaven. This is our prayer.

Rev. Peter G. Jankowski

27th Sunday in Ordinary Time (Is 5: 1-7; Ps 80: 9-12, 13-14, 15-16, 19-20; Phil 4: 6-9; Mt 21: 33-43)

Recently, I had an opportunity to celebrate the wedding between a couple named Jeff and Christina. About 30-35 times a year, I have the opportunity to celebrate the sacrament of marriage with the couples of our parish and get a chance to get to know more closely about 50-60 people of our parish in the process. Meeting with the couples is important to me; I want to learn how the couples first met and grew in God's love together. I want to get the couples to ask questions about their relationship. I have found, statistically, that the more the couples ask questions prior to marriage, the better the chance that the marriage will work out.

About a month before the wedding, I get the bride and the groom to plan the wedding with me and as part of the process, I get the couple to write "love letters" about each other – why is the relationship important, why they love their partner, write down stories about their relationship.

So I was given the pleasure to read these love letters and I learned how Jeff and Christina grew in their friendship by taking strolls down the river walk in a neighboring town. The couple told us how they spent time together talking on the computer, spending time in college together and yes, those river walks.

As I listened to these stories, I was thinking about this image that has been going through my mind awhile, an image that reflects the love of a marriage or of any vocation in general. I was thinking about someone taking a walk by this river and getting into a boat. You take someone with you, someone you truly love and you begin sailing down this river in the boat. Here is the key to this relationship. You take those oars in the boat and you throw them into the water. You pull down the sail, turn off the motor, throw them all into the water and allow the boat to casually drift down the water. It is at that point that you realize, metaphorically speaking, that the only one you need to guide the boat is God and all you want to do is sit in the boat, enjoy the experience of life and share it with the person who means the most to you.

For those of you who are married, it is that life partner of yours with whom you choose to share that boat. I truly respect a person that makes that kind of life-commitment. They make a decision to give up all kinds of things in life so that they can completely devote their lives to that one special person.

Then there is a person like me and all those priests and religious out there who ride in the boat as well. We, too, have chosen to give up many things in life so that we can focus on the one. But our choice is not one person but one community instead. We choose not to take care of one individual but instead take care of all of you through prayer and service. You are the spouse. We are the spouse. Christ is our groom and we are His bride. When we ride the boat, we share that experience together, each of us called to minister to each other in our own unique way, based on the talents we have been given.

But as we know, this trip is going to be difficult. It is hard for anyone to allow someone to steer the boat instead of ourselves. We want control of our lives. We want control in the things that we do. The only problem is, when we allow anything else to steer the boat except God, we end up drifting and going into directions that make us lose focus.

We learn in marriage formation that if a couple puts God in the center of their life, if they go to Church together, if they tithe and celebrate natural family planning and put their family first, the odds of them staying together and extremely good. Those who do not, those who put up the sail and control their own lives, end up having other foundations in life that are do not bind them with their spouse. Then, when there is a valley in the relationship, it is then that a couple especially need God in their relationship and without that foundation, the couple often drifts apart.

The readings we hear this weekend are the same ones that Jeff and Christina chose for their wedding this weekend. Jeff and Christina made a commitment yesterday (today) to make the two become one, to share their experience in the boat. The goal of all vocations is to allow God into that relationship and to let God guide our relationships. Let us always make God first in all that we do. Let us share this experience with the one who created us and gives us life. That is how we build a relationship with God. That is how we pray today.

28th Sunday in Ordinary Time (Is 25: 6-10a; Ps 23: 1-3a, 3b-4, 5, 6; Phil 4: 12-14, 19-20; Mt 22: 1-14 or 22: 1-10)

I was reading an article from <u>The Reader's Digest</u> some time ago concerning a bunch of people who tried to climb Mt. Everest. I read that this task is a daunting one, something that only a person with either great determination or foolishness would attempt. In the article, I read that three quarters of the way up the mountain, a station was erected for the benefit of the climbers, a station which housed oxygen tanks and extra equipment which a climber might need.

The thing is, that last station is the last respite of hope for the climber. Once the climber leaves the station, there is no way for anyone to rescue the person before they reach the top of the mountain. If a climber breaks their leg past this point or encounters some other debilitating injury, no one can help that person and no one can rescue them. There are stories about people who have died climbing the mountain and whose bodies are still lodged up on the mountain.[xlvi]

With that image in mind, I read this week's readings and I started to think about the wedding banquet resting on the top of that mountain. I thought about the celebration God holds on the mountain, with the finest food and drink, with the greatest friends, with all the things we would ever want in life. The feast at the top of the mountain is extremely desirable, something that we all strive to have. The problem is, in order to celebrate the feast with God, *we must first climb the mountain.*

I often wonder how hard it is for any of us to make it up that mountain. Every time we try to climb, we often get bogged down by indifference or temptation or some type of obstacle that gets in our way. I wonder what it would be like for the people of the world who, like in today's gospel, are invited to this wedding banquet before us, but yet they refuse to come. Like the people in the gospel, there are often other, more pressing matters in their lives, matters like their farms or their jobs or football games or practices.

I wonder what it would be like if people thought they could climb the mountain alone. I wonder if these people would follow the advice of people like the fifth century heretic Pelagius, who stated that we can make it up the mountain without God's help. Yet, as hard as we try, there is no way we make it up the mountain this way. When we try to climb the mountain alone, we end up carrying the load of sin on our backs that weigh us down too much and make it impossible to climb.

The only way we make it up that mountain is through the help of God and the Christian people around us. When we pray for each other, serve each other and share this meal at the table with each other, we support the people of the world and we give them strength. When we pray to God and God gives us this gift of His word and sacrament, we find strength to make it up the hill.

The challenge in our lives is to ask ourselves if we are even making an attempt to climb the mountain so that we can join in the banquet. I have stated over the last few weeks that my personal goal in this parish is that every family do one thing to promote the kingdom of God and build this faith. It seems that after two thousand years we have come a long way, but based on what we see in Church every Sunday, I also know we have a long way to go.

Let us serve each other, love each other, take care of each other and climb that mountain together. This is our prayer.

29th Sunday in Ordinary Time (Is 45: 1, 4-6; Ps 96: 1-3, 4-5, 7-8, 9-10; 1 Th 1: 1-5b; Mt 22: 15-21)

Around this time each year Mother Church celebrates her yearly anniversary of the First Formal Meeting of Bishops at the Second Vatican Council. The Holy Father at the time, St. Pope John XXIII (who has often been called, "the good pope"), had just been elected as Holy Father just a few years earlier as what many at the time considered a "transitional" time. Many pundits saw John XXIII as a man who would serve as a caretaker of this divine office after the long run of his two predecessors, Pope Pius XI (1922-1939) and Pope Pius XII (1939-1958). Many saw John XXIII as a gentle, loving, holy man. Personally, I have prayed to our Lord that I might somehow be able to emulate the man's heart; unfortunately, the only thing I emulate is his girth...

This "good pope" felt that the time had arisen to uphold and re-present the will of God to a people who had evolved and changed since these issues of faith were addressed at an Ecumenical council some 400 years earlier. As he stated at the beginning of the council:

> The greatest concern of the ecumenical council is this: that the sacred deposit of Christian doctrine be guarded and taught more effectively.[xlvii]

St. Pope John XXIII wrote these words, I suspect, to narrow the gulf that existed between those of the Catholic faith and those of other Christian and non-Christian faith traditions, that all of us, created in the image and likeness of God, have the responsibility of seeking out the good that unites us rather than the differences that divide us. Good, St. Pope John XXIII began a process that took five years, the lifespan of another Holy Father and far beyond to complete. Vatican II's task of promoting and defending God's will in today's age helped the modern faithful understand Mother Church in a language and a way of living that we could understand and, in many ways, have made us a better and more accepting and loving Church because of it.

That said, a member of our community approached me with a theological question I have to address periodically at St. Patrick's, a question that I have to address quite frequently in my classes at the university: "How beneficial was the Second Vatican Council to the faithful of today's age?"

I am asked that question because, like most documents that are written in life, the intention of the author seems to get lost as soon as the document leaves the author's hands. We are taught this in our literature classes: how often do book clubs and internet chat rooms discuss the significance of the words of a text that often go well beyond the intention of the author (good or bad), as if the words of a text take a life of their own?

In the world of politics (God help me if my brother hears me talking politics), I became a bit distraught when New York Mayor Michael Bloomberg held a memorial service on the 10th Anniversary of the World Trade Center Bombings but did not involve one leader of any faith nor mentioned one spiritual reference at this memorial service. I become distraught when politicos and even the media begin some type of fear campaign against people of today's age based off the faith traditions they choose to live. The practice is called "Theophobia" (or a fear of the Church), a lifestyle determined to scare people away from a faith in a country whose founding principles are faith-based.

Of the myriads of quotations that I could utilize in discussing these issues, I came across two that I thought were quite relevant for the sake of this homily. The first came from George Washington, who wrote the following to Colonel Burwell Bassett on April 25, 1773 at a time just prior to the American Revolution. Washington wrote,

> The ways of Providence being inscrutable and the justice of it not to be scanned by the shallow eye of humanity, nor to be counteracted by the utmost efforts of human power or wisdom, resignation and as far as the strength of our reason and religion can carry us, a cheerful acquiescence to the Divine Will, is what we are to aim.[xlviii]

The second reference comes from President Abraham Lincoln during his formal proclamation of Thanksgiving as a National Holiday on October 3, 1863. President Lincoln writes,

> To these bounties, which are so constantly enjoyed that we are prone to forget the source from which

they come, others have been added which are of so extraordinary a nature that they cannot fail to penetrate and soften even the heart which is habitually insensible to the ever-watchful providence of Almighty God.

...No human counsel hath devised nor hath any mortal hand worked out these great things. They are the gracious gifts of the Most High God, who, while dealing with us in anger for our sins, hath nevertheless remembered mercy.[xlix]

With all due regard to the First Amendment, those of faith understand clearly that the life we have been given is a gift from God, freely offered to us in love. Our response to this gift, our response to God, is a choice completely of our own making and not controlled by our Lord at any moment. As we have learned in sacred scripture, *we chose* to leave the Garden of Eden and *we chose* to build the Tower of Babel. *We chose* to follow God out of the land of Egypt, that place of slavery into the Promised Land. *We chose* whether we wished to keep the Promised Land or whether we wished God to remove us from it due to our actions, good or bad. Certainly in this age, *we choose* the manner in which we live in this country, whether we choose to give to Caesar, to God, or to find a way to balance the two in our lives.

As Washington, Lincoln and the various other Christian leaders in our country have written, by welcoming those of other faith traditions and of other cultures, we have become a richer, more accepting and more loving people in the process. With God's help and our own choosing, we have learned, to some degree, that these inalienable rights of life, liberty and the pursuit of happiness do not exist for just one people but for *all* peoples. Perhaps this is the reason why the Protestant acceptance of Catholic Maryland in the 17th century paved the way for our own free expression of the Catholic faith throughout the entire country. Perhaps if we learn how to "give back to God" in the way we treat each human being that God creates, then we understand the true meaning of today's gospel, which goes far beyond the notion of taxes and money.

About three years ago in reflecting on the Church's spiritual life in the country of France, Pope Benedict XVI reflected on the relationship between God and the secular life during one of his General Audiences that took place on September 17th. The Holy Father spoke these words on this subject:

> ... if the image of Caesar was stamped on Roman coins which for this reason were to be rendered to him, the human heart bears the imprint of the Creator, the one Lord of our life. Genuine secularism does not mean, therefore, leaving the spiritual dimension out of consideration but rather recognizing that it is precisely this that radically guarantees our freedom and autonomy from earthly realities, thanks to the dictates of creative Wisdom which the human conscience is capable of accepting and actuating.[l]

Give to Caesar what is Caesar but to God what is God's.[li] Give thanks to God on the blessings you have been given and make sure that this blessing is imprinted on the human heart so that our heart becomes God's heart and that God's heart may be shared with others. It's a rather nice message to learn from today's gospel and certainly puts the writings and reasons for the Vatican II documents in perspective.

On the eve of the first meeting of the Second Vatican Council, St. Pope John XXIII stood outside the window on his papal balcony and offered these words of love that very much fulfill the heart of today's scripture readings. I would like to conclude my homily with these words today:

My own person counts for nothing -- it's a brother who speaks to you, became a father by the will of our Lord, but all together, fatherhood and brotherhood and God's grace, give honor to the impressions of this night, which are always our feelings, which now we express before heaven and earth: faith, hope, love, love of God, love of brother, all aided along the way in the Lord's holy peace for the work of the good. So, let us continue to love each other, to look out for each other along the way: to welcome whoever comes close to us and set aside whatever difficulty it might bring.

When you head home, find your children. Hug and kiss your children and tell them: 'This is the hug and kiss of the Pope.' When you find them with tears to dry, give them a good word. Give anyone who suffers a word of comfort. Tell them 'The Pope is with us especially in our times of sadness and bitterness.' Then, all together, may we always come alive -- whether to sing, to breathe, or to cry, but always full of trust in Christ, who helps us and hears us, let us continue along our path.[lii]

This is our prayer.

30th Sunday in Ordinary Time (Ex 22: 20-26; Ps 18: 2-3a, 3b-4, 47-51; 1 Th 1: 5c-10; Mt 22: 34-40)

When I went to junior high school, I used to think I was pretty hot stuff on the trombone. I had studied band music practically all my life – when I was in first grade, I wanted to play the T-bone, but the music teacher told me my arms were not long enough to get past fourth position on the instrument. I didn't care, though. For eight years, I wanted to be the best at that instrument, better than anyone else.

So there I was in the eighth grade, sitting in the first chair trombone section, thinking I was pretty hot stuff. I went to all the special band camps and conferences and I was always picked to do all that important kind of band stuff.

But no matter how good I thought I was, there was someone who sat right in front of me that made me jealous. The guy was named Ron and he was a saxophone player. He wasn't the cleanest looking of people, he didn't look like he washed his hair and he always wore cowboy boots and a furry coat, something that made him the object of ridicule. He tried to make friends, but he often annoyed people enough that no one liked to talk to him, including me.

Yet, as much as he was ridiculed, Ron had a gift that surpassed all of us. By far, Ron was the best musician in the group. He played better than any of us and he could do without blinking the things that took years for me to achieve. The thing that drove me the most nuts was that *he couldn't read a note of music!* I heard that there are people that possess this particular musical gift, most notably Eric Clapton, Eddie Van Halen nor any of the Beatles. But I never thought I would sit in a class with someone like that. I was ticked that a teen who was so despised had such a gift in life.

The problem with many of us is that we don't take time to realize how special the people sitting next to us actually are. In fact, as I sit in the confessional listening to others, I think about those who might drive me crazy, those who we might not consider very important but who probably are the most important people in the kingdom of heaven.

The bishops of the Second Vatican council understood that the gift of life is sacred and the gifts that each of us possess are like puzzle pieces that help us become more whole in our faith life. The council wrote in the Pastoral Constitution, *The Church in the Modern World (Gaudium et Spes),*

... Everyone must consider his every neighbor without exception as another self, taking into account first of all His life and the means necessary to living it with dignity, so as not to imitate the rich man who had no concern for the poor man Lazarus.[liii]

In our times a special obligation binds us to make ourselves the neighbor of every person without exception and of actively helping him when he comes across our path, whether he be an old person abandoned by all, a foreign laborer unjustly looked down upon, a refugee, a child born of an unlawful union and wrongly suffering for a sin he did not commit, or a hungry person who disturbs our conscience by recalling the voice of the Lord, "As long as you did it for one of these the least of my brethren, you did it for me" (Matt. 25: 40).[liv]

The minute we despise anyone, the minute we stop loving is the moment that we abandon our faith. Christ tells us in the gospel that not only do we have to tolerate those we don't like, we must love them with the same vigor that we love the neighbors that we like. We must do for others as God does for us, since we probably abuse God more often on a daily basis than anyone else probably abuses us.

Today is the day for change and reform. Today is the day to learn how to love every person that we meet, especially those like "Saxophone Ron," who possess so many gifts that we often cannot comprehend. It is the simplest message of our faith and yet the most profound- love God and love each other. Let us love today. Let us take care of each other. Let us learn about the gifts that others possess so that we can learn from them and learn about God. This is our prayer.

31st Sunday in Ordinary Time (Mal 1: 14b—2: 2b, 8-10; Ps 131: 1, 2, 3; 1 Th 2: 7b-9, 13; Mt 23: 1-12)

The inspiraton for today's homily comes from a sin that I committed last week on a Monday afternoon, a sin that some might not consider so bad to others but I consider myself as something very detrimental to my faith. The sin took place just before I was preparing myself to take my afternoon nap. A former pastor once taught me that for every three parts to a day (morning, afternoon and evening), a healthy priest should take one of the three parts off for the sake of rest, to re-energize the batteries for the sake of the faithful that I serve in the parish. The previous weekend for me was very long; I celebrated the Masses, I visited the sick and I did all the things a parish priest would do for his own local community. My sometimes mischievous basset hound had woken me up the previous evening because he does not follow the same set schedule that I choose to live and I couldn't get back to sleep after my dog Rusty paid a visit to Mother Nature outdoors. Prior to my siesta, I was teaching at the university that night and I really needed to get some good rest for the sake of my sanity.

Then I received the afternoon phone call. Somehow the call slipped passed the secretary and made its way up to my room.

The call came from a nurse in the Emergency Room of a local hospital, a nurse who told me that she had called every priest in the city for help and no one was available. To be honest with you, these words are not comforting to me – sometimes people tell me this line when, in fact, no other priest has been called and besides, when someone tells me that I am the *last* person on their list that they wanted to call, I usually do not get all warm and fuzzy in my response. Nevertheless, I got up from my afternoon siesta and responded to her request. I figure that I am a priest and, to a point, if a child in my care is in a critical situation I should *want* to take care of her or him. I certainly would think that the person in critical condition would be thinking that way, too.

As I dressed myself and drove to the hospital, there was a chorus of anger playing music in my head. It was a this point that my great sin took place: *Road Rage.* It did not matter that no one around me was actually driving badly. At that moment, every car I passed seemed like an enemy that stood between me and my sleep. I was furious at the nurse, I was furious at the patient and I was furious at every priest in the two or three cities that laid in the path between the hospital and my own parish. As I reached the hospital, I had terrible thoughts racing through my mind about this hospital resident who did nothing except ask for the graces of a sacrament during a time of trial. I actually had to take a deep breath and compose myself before I entered the room and met this focus of all my pent-up anger.

However, as soon as I entered the hospital emergency room on that Monday afternoon, my disposition seemed to change. In plain sight in front of me stood one of our beloved Poor Clare sisters, a religious who has spent decades of her life praying for people like you and me. For the first time in many a year, I encounterd Mother Superior out of her conclave, as the Poor Clares take a vow of cloister within their community (I sometimes forget that the sisters exist below the torso, as I usually encounter them on the other side of a partition will covers their bottom half!). What a blessing I encountered by praying the Salve Regina with the community in the Emergency Room and offering the Sacrament of the Sick to someone so precious.

As I came to the end of my visit with them, the Poor Clares very graciously thanked me for my ministry. In my heart, I was much more grateful that the sisters ministered to the priest and made this sinner realize the reason I became a priest in the first place – to offer the presence of Christ to the believer and to see that presence of Christ in the *heart* of the believer.

Do and observe all things whatsoever they tell you, but do not follow their example – these words rang so true in the life of a sinful priest from last week and in a sense, they ring true for all of us today. Concerning every priest or believer that walks into this room, you may appreciate some qualities any of them may possess. There may be other qualities that you may not appreciate. But the fact is, if our ministry is based on the individual rather than the *presence of Christ* within the individual, then our ministry may seemed somewhat misplaced.

What makes my ministry such a joy is that not only do I have the opportunity to serve each individual sitting in this room, but I also have the joy of seeing the presence of God *within* each individual. A lot of the times, I might forget about the presence of God that is within my own heart, but when I serve others, the God I see in their hearts reflects the same God that rests within me. The more I serve, the more I realize how special a gift our Lord is within my heart, for which I give great thanks. This is not possible without investing myself in Christian service. This is not possible without serving the ones that Christ has called me to serve. In the ministry of the priests, bishops, deacons and religious, we are able to understand our Lord in a deeper way through you, in the way you seek out the Lord in the sacraments and share your faith with others in the community.

On your part, I would hope that you could see through the individual that serves you and see the God that is serving through the minister. The reason we offer special respect to the priest at Mass is not necessarily because the individual has special gifts (the fact is that the gifts were offered to the individual by our Lord in the first place). The reason we offer respect is because when we enter into the life of faith with the right disposition, we are able to look through the priest in order to see the Lord that dwells *within* that minister. With that disposition properly focused, we realize that is the *Lord* who confers the sacraments, the Lord who speaks to us, the Lord who offers us grace and forgiveness, made visible in the sight of the priest.

If nothing else today, we should remember that if our lives are dependent on people like Pete Jankowski, then we are going to fail because Pete Jankowski is not the teacher; Pete Jankowski is a sinner who needs to be guided by the true teacher as well. If our lives are dependent on the Jesus Christ who shines *through* Fr. Pete Jankowski, then our dependency is properly placed and we are properly disposed to approach the priest so that we can find the grace that we speak. If we understand this difference, this nuance, then we are well on our way to the road to heaven. For that reason among others, I am so grateful that we change the response to the simple greeting "The Lord be with you" to the response, "With your Spirit," as the ministry that is offered through me should not be seen as given by me but rather by Christ's Spirit that work's through me.

Let us give thanks for the men and woman who have allowed themselves to be vessels for Christ. Let us strive to be vessels for Christ ourselves, in whatever path of life God has directed us to follow. Let us show this presence of Christ to the people that we meet and let us see this presence of Christ in the hearts of those we serve. This is our prayer.

32nd Sunday in Ordinary Time (Wis 6: 12-16; Ps 63: 2, 3-4, 5-6, 7-8; 1 Th 4: 13-18 or 4: 13-14; Mt 25: 1-13)

Today I would like to introduce you to a new word in your English vocabulary: *chundolay*. You may have never heard this word before, mostly because it is a made up one. I learned this word from a seminary classmate of mine named Bob from twenty or so years ago. When things went wrong in his life, when he felt like getting angry and saying things that should not be said, Bob refused to swear or hurt anyone so he would use this word to express his dissatisfaction in life - *chundolay*.

I thought about this word recently after reflecting on the three gospel readings from Matthew that conclude this year's liturgical year. I suppose that the gospel writers could easily have skipped the twenty-fifth chapter of Matthew's gospel from which these three readings come and jump right to the end of the book, where the last lines of the text are filled with hope and inspiration: "Go and make disciples of the nations. Baptize them in the name of the Father and of the Son and of the Holy Spirit. Teach that what I have commanded you. And know that I am with you always until the end of the age."[lv] But as is said concerning the world of music, the only way to get to Carnegie Hall is to "practice, practice, practice"; the only way to heaven is to "love, love, love," always in God's name.

Here is the problem for me. In this society and certainly in this parish, I am often asked to preach the "Good News" to the faithful, even though the scripture readings often see the need to present a dual message of the faith rather than focus on solely the positive. For every Old Testament story about a patient and loving God in Exodus who stands by the side of a chosen people in a time of distress, we also encounter a more vengeful and warning God in the books of Kings and many of the prophets that shows us what happens for those who do not live the faith. Every time in our gospel readings that we hear about the joys of gathering around this banquet table for a feast beyond compare for those who possess faith, we also hear the stories of what happens to those who disregard the feast altogether. By working our way through the bible, God's message to us becomes crystal clear – if you stay obedient to the Lord's path and love with all your heart and soul our God and God's Church then an eternal life awaits you. If not... *chundolay.*

Rev. Peter G. Jankowski

Over these next three weeks, this theme becomes evidently clear through the words our Lord presents us. I have practically memorized the message from today's gospel, as I utilize it at practically every quinceañera service I offer at this parish and throughout the diocese during my last fifteen years of priesthood. The message becomes a great catechetical moment in the tradition of the Mexican people, who celebrate this feast of "the fifteenth birthday" of a young woman's life, called a *quinceañera*. As we understand this tradition, the celebration used to symbolize a young woman's passage into motherhood, a time when she would pass through the age of innocence and move into adulthood. After the Spanish occupation some 500 years ago, the celebration changed its focus. Taken into a Christian context, the focus of this celebration shifted towards a prayer to our Blessed Mother, a time when a young woman devoted herself to be an outstanding example of holiness and care for her family as Mary was to hers.

On the day of her quinceañera, the teenage girl enters the church dressed in a white veil and escorted by her family in friends. In the context of Mass, this young woman offers a prayer of dedication to Mary and receives gifts from her family, symbols that reflect the family's loyalty to this person. As we open the scriptures to read the gospel passage, we usually turn to one that we read today, a text that instructs the woman about the responsibilities of keeping God ever present in her life, as opposed to a life empty of the oil of faith. If she is vigilant, if the lamp is full of oil, then she will be prepared to receive Christ in her life. If not, if she falls asleep when the time arrives for the bridegroom's entrance, then she will be left behind.

This image of the empty jar of oil is extremely important to the faith life of a fifteen-year-old Mexican girl and it is an important image for those of us sitting here today. When we share our faith, when we continue to build our relationship with God, God continually pours oil into our jars. The love never stops; it continues to pour into our lives. The more we look at God and see this love, it seems like we have fallen in love all over again.

But as with all relationships, this love for God takes work. Every couple I have talked to tells me that they continually adjust their relationship in order to maintain their love. Priests need continually to pray and draw closer to God in order for their ministry to be effective. All this year, the gospel of Matthew has told us that the call to discipleship requires us to a whole lot more than we could ever imagine, from accepting God's invitation to this wedding banquet every Sunday to loving our neighbor and God with all of our heart. As we say about Carnegie Hall, the only way to get there is to "practice, practice, practice"; as we say about the faith, the only way we get to heaven is to "love, love, love," always in God's name.

The message of our gospel readings these next three weeks is clear: whenever we put our faith in things other than God, we become drained and begin to lose hope. The jar begins to lose its oil. Think about it- how many times have any of us said, "Well, I'd love to go to Church but I have to mow the lawn or visit friends or pay my bills," or some other excuse? When the king invites us to the wedding of his son, do we come to the wedding, or do we have something better to do that the church defines as an "inferior activity," a term that Mother Church associates with grave sin in the context of skipping Mass? When we are commissioned at the end of Mass to serve other people, do we put down what we are doing and help others out or does selfishness become more important than a total self-giving of others?

In my reflection of this "dual message" we constantly hear within our faith lives, I understand more clearly what the concept of "the fear of the Lord" really means for those who attach the word "Catholic" to their names. Yes, we can understand this gift of the Spirit as a punishing-type "reckoning" that awaits those who abandon the faith – I believe today's gospel calls this type of life a "wailing and grinding of teeth" to which God responds, "Amen – it is as if I never knew you." But for those who live the faith, know and live their prayers and come to Mass to share in this meal, the fear can be seen as a type of love infinitely more intimate than staring into your loved one's eyes and falling so deeply in love with God that you never want to look away. The bottle of faith becomes so full that it overflows with God's presence and what results is a trembling on our part that is so deep with love that we become engrossed in a love that we never want to end. <u>That</u> is the Good News from today's gospel message and <u>that</u> is what gives us hope in the readings we encounter these last three weeks of this liturgical year.

Today, let us see the goodness of God that flows within us, a love that refreshes us and allows us to see how this loving God really was in this world. Let us never fall asleep and forget this love. Let us permit others to offer God's love to us and let us offer that love to others. Let us bring this love to the altar, receive God's body and blood into our lives and share God with the people that we meet. This is our prayer today.

33rd Sunday in Ordinary Time (Pr 31: 10-13, 19-20, 30-31; Ps 128: 1-2, 3, 4-5; 1 Th 5: 1-6; Mt 25: 14-30 or 25: 14-15, 19-21)

As part of my own spiritual formation, I have spent a good deal of time these last few months teaching a couple of college level courses at the University of St. Francis. At first, I thought the courses would prove overwhelming to my schedule, which, at times, they certainly are. But I have found most recently that the classes have become quite therapeutic to me, as they have given me the opportunity to reflect on my own faith life and share it with a group of students who seek to understand the basic tenets of the Catholic faith. In the whole of my teaching experiences since the beginning of this school year, I have found that this challenge has presented itself in many venues, whether it be challenging our own grade school kids about their knowledge of the commandments and the precepts of the Church or students in a higher institution of learning who return back to these same commandments and precepts later in life.

In the online course I have been teaching this week, I posed a question to my college students that very much parallels the theme to today's scripture readings. The question I posed to them is as follows: "What ritual experience, religious or not, have you yourself had that made a deep impression on you? Can you explain why?" One of my students, a woman named Carol, presented the group with the following answer...

> The ritual that I have seen that made a deep impression on me was while I was at work as a nursing supervisor in a convent. When one of the Sisters dies it is announced on the overhead paging system. If you happen to be on the floor where the death has happened, you will see 15-20 sisters come walking down the hall (to the room of the sister who is dying). They all come together to pray and celebrate that this Sister has gone to God. The first time I saw it I had goose bumps.
>
> The other ritual that happens is when a Sister is actively dying. Sisters can sign up for a specific time and then go and sit with the Sister. They do this so the Sister is not alone. If they want, the other Sisters will sit with them and take time to pray, talk, play music, etc. Both of these rituals have made an impact on me because I see the Sisters coming together when it is a time of sorrow for most individuals, but when I see their response to the death it is usually one of joy because the Sister has gone to God. When I personally think about the loss of a loved one it is usually with sorrow because I will miss them.

What surprised Carol during this time of grief was the level of celebration a group of nuns would have at a time that our society often views as one of sadness. In my reflection of the readings this week and the conversations in which the students from all levels have engaged, I came to the conclusion that if a person truly invests their lives into a sacred purpose, then they realize what their higher purpose serves in this world and that entering into the world of our higher calling becomes a moment of joy instead of sorrow. For those who invest their talents in the world of faith, whether those talents may be small or large, what comes back in return in greater than an economy can ever offer us. What we get back in return is an everlasting life of peace with God, a life that doesn't fluctuate like a stock market but is constant and full of love and will last for the rest of our existence. *For this reason,* I believe the sisters find reason to celebrate during the time of death for one of their own.

When I reflected on Carol's response, I reminded myself about the writings of one of St. Pope John Paul II's favorite theologians, Cardinal Hans Urs von Balthasar, who wrote a reader's digest version of his teachings for "Dick and Jane" theologians like me. The work is called *A Resume of My Thought,* which reduces his teachings to a simple gaze into the eyes of a person that you love. This is probably the easiest image that we can have when it comes to understanding the presence of the divine in our lives.

For Balthasar, if you truly love someone and wish to enter into their life, all you have to do is constantly gaze into their eyes with love. Now if I chose at this Mass to stare into the eyes of someone in this community, one of two things might happen. Most likely, the person into whose eyes I am staring will probably think to themselves, "this priest is out of his cuckoo and I wish he would get away from me" (and by the way, this would be the most proper and appropriate response, *because I'm nuts*)." For the person who does not love you, this gaze can seem uncomfortable and very much unwanted.

But if you are in love with someone, the gaze is not just appropriate – *it is desired* – for this gaze can lead to the most intimate moments that two people in love can ever experience. St. Augustine compares the relationship of the Father and the Son to the love that binds two people deeply, infinitely in love, where the concept of love parallels itself to the work of the Holy Spirit. Every time two people fall in love, they reflect (in some small way) to the relationship of the Lover and the Beloved, united together by love itself.

Because we are not in a seminary or institution of higher learning, most of us in this Church probably can understand the divine most clearly in this way – to understand God is to stare in His eyes in the same way that the Son of God stares lovingly into the eyes of His Father. To use fancy twenty-five cent theological jargon, Balthasar writes the following:

> We add here that the epiphany of being has sense only if in the appearance (*Erscheinung*) we grasp the essence which manifests itself (*Ding an sich*). The infant comes to the knowledge not of a pure appearance, but of his mother in herself. That does not exclude our grasping the essence only through the manifestation and not in itself (St. Thomas).[lvi]

To put this in terms that even I can understand, I find this passage to mean that most of us in this community are not the highly intellectual theologians that can go on "*Ding an sich-ing*" all day long and reflect on the essence of a thing in itself *(in se)*. We in the parish setting, though, are not generally theologians; we are the "moms and pops" of the world, the workers of the vineyard and we experience our God in the things that we say and the things that we do. We are the faithful who can see the presence of God when we gaze into the lives of our kids and in our parents. We are the faithful who watch a kid grow up, see how they act and live their life and often say to ourselves, "that kid acts just like their father and mother."

We are the generation that realizes that to understand Christ, we have to act like Christ. We are the kind of people who can better understand Christ when we can say to ourselves, "that person acts just like Christ when they contribute to the Food Pantry, when they minister to the sick, when they invest in the life of the parish (this is the theme for next week's reading). The more we live like Christ and invest ourselves in the Christ-like life we live, then we realize how the five talents we put in multiply into ten, twenty and thirty fold by the grace that comes forth from our actions. *This* is how I perceive Balthasar's understanding of *Erscheinung* – this is the kind of Christ-like appearance that we faithful in the parish choose to live.

Balthasar continues,

> As the Son in God is the eternal icon of the Father, he can without contradiction assume in himself the

image that is the creation, purify it and make it enter into the communion of the divine life without dissolving it (in a false mysticism). It is here that one must distinguish nature and grace.[lvii]

In this passage, I come to realize that every time we gaze into the life of the Son, we thereby gaze into the life of the Father. If we wish to understand the one who ultimately created us and gave us this soul, we must engage ourselves in the life of the *Erscheinung* by living like Christ, by loving like Christ and by gazing into the icon of Christ, who serves as the window and image of His Father in heaven.

But as I learned from my students in the university class I teach, if we stand too far back in this exercise and choose not to invest ourselves in the life of faith, if we distance ourselves too much, then we are like the worker who buried his talents into the ground. By trying to offend no one or by doing nothing at all, we tend not to connect with anyone.

We are one week away from the end of our liturgical year and this Season in Ordinary Time. In these last two weeks, St. Matthew's gospel becomes quite harsh in the way we are evaluated by God, connecting our salvation to the Christ-like manner that we choose to live on earth. For those who invest in the faith and act like Christ, this life of the *Erscheinung* serves as the key to our entry into the kingdom of heaven. For those who do not, St. Matthew becomes quite clear, as we will find out in next week's gospel reading.

Let us use these readings from Matthew's gospel as both a warning and a challenge as to how we need to conduct ourselves and live this Catholic life. The real sadness of life results from the person who loves. As Carol experienced in her life as a convent nurse, the person who experiences Christ will find joy even at the moment of death, for death serves as a bridge between an imperfect life on earth and the life of perfection that awaits those who constantly gaze into the life of love. Let us gaze into this life together and live this Christ-like life together as a community of faith. Let us be an *Erscheinung* people together. This is our prayer.

34th Sunday in Ordinary Time - *Christ the King* (Ez 34: 11-12, 15-17; Ps 23: 1-2a, 2b-3, 5, 6; 1 Cor 15: 20-26, 28; Mt 25: 31-46)

On Saturday morning, a couple members of our parish and I attended one of those long diocesan meetings that was very important to attend but very inconvenient for a priest who had a long day of work ahead of him. By the end of the meeting I was already allotting time for each remaining task I had to complete that day, as all of the tasks were necessary for the well-being of the parish.

As I rushed out of the meeting heading back to the parish for baptisms, I couldn't help but notice that the powers of heaven conveniently inserted a McDonald's restaurant right on my way back. Because I didn't have time to eat breakfast in the morning, I decided to take advantage of the stop.

The first thing I noticed at the McDonald's counter was an advertisement for the seasonal "McRib" Sandwich that the company periodically offers during the year. The advertising hit its mark – I was tempted to buy the product. The only problem was that earlier in the week, I read an article from the internet concerning what the company actually uses to make this sauce dripping lunchtime meal. I read the following from my Yahoo! server:

What is the McRib made of? (It is made of) pig innards and plenty of salt. Typically, "restructured meat product" includes pig bits like tripe, heart and scalded stomach... These parts are cooked and blended with salt and water to extract salt-soluble proteins, which act as a "glue" that helps bind the reshaped meat together. (The McRib is) ... certainly not good for you. Though "slightly trimmer than the Big Mac," ... the McRib... still packs in 500 calories and 26 grams of fat.[lviii]

So do you think I bought the McRib Sandwich? *Of course I did!!!* If nothing else in life, I have learned that the small obstacles in life like nutritional value and doctor's warnings are ever going to stop me from purchasing those things that I want to eat. Of course, five years (or possibly five hours) from now, I probably will be back here at Mass, explaining to you the dangers of eating unhealthy food in the same way someone who is addicted to cigarettes or some other vice would do the same if they were suffering from their compulsions or addictions.

In this light, I started thinking about those other types of foods that I really enjoy eating, knowing that the foods I eat have practically no nutritional value. Take "The Twinkie." I used to joke that the kingdom of heaven was like a Twinkie at a convenience store because the Twinkie seemingly has an eternal shelf life – it will taste just as horribly years down the line as it does today. The same goes for "Mrs. Fischer's" potato chips from Rockford, IL. In my heart of hearts, I know the secret of their recipe – you throw the potato chips in the fryer, *you turn the fryer on and* you only take them out until every drop of cholesterol-dripping lard is soaked into the chips.

So if we know that something is bad for us to eat and we eat it anyway, why do we do this? Why do we commit ourselves to eating it? In the same light, if we know that a certain act is sinful and then we commit the sin anyway, what is our motivation for doing to sin? Why would we commit an act that separates ourselves from the presence of God and our Church?

The gospel of Matthew has made the answer to these questions rather clear to us this last year, as we celebrate the final week of the season in Ordinary Time. The answer is based on the fact that we all are fragile and weak human beings, dependent on a king to guide us in the proper direction that we need to live. Especially in Matthew, we are taught that a new king, this "anointed" Messiah, would reestablish properly our relationship to God and redirect us in the manner in which we should live. We have been taught that where we human beings often give in to temptation to sin, this king would be resolved to turn away from sin and present to us the gospel message. We learn that the motivation for this king is based on nothing else but love... and love is the theme of our gospel and of this homily today.

Notice over the last three weeks, the focus on Matthew's gospel directs itself towards those who pursue a life of love and those who choose to live against it. For those who serve and love and clothe and feed those who are needy in God's name, the great heavenly treasure awaits; for those who do not, they will experience a wailing and a grinding of teeth. For those who live the life of God, they realize their purpose and reason for the life they have been given and live out that life to the full; for those who do not, who perpetually live their life as if they were eating one McRib Sandwich after another, no earthly doctor will be able to cure what plagues that person spiritually.

In that light, I thought about Pope Benedict's first encyclical he wrote as a Holy Father, *Deus Caritas Est (God is love)*. In this encyclical, our Holy Father based his work off the writings of the first letter of St. John in the New Testament, whose theme focuses on how the righteous should learn the lessons from those who have strayed from the faith and have lost their way in their pursuit to build a relationship with God. At the very beginning of his encyclical, the Holy Father writes,

> "God is love and he who abides in love abides in God and God abides in him" (*1 Jn* 4: 16). These words from the *First Letter of John* express with remarkable clarity the heart of the Christian faith: the Christian image of God and the resulting image of mankind and its destiny. In the same verse, Saint John also offers a kind of summary of the Christian life: "We have come to know and to believe in the love God has for us."

We have come to believe in God's love: in these words, the Christian can express the fundamental decision of his life... Saint John's Gospel describes that event in these words: "God so loved the world that He gave His Only Son, that whoever believes in Him should ... have eternal life" (3: 16). In acknowledging the centrality of love, Christian faith has retained the core of Israel's faith, while at the same time giving it new depth and breadth. The pious Jew prayed daily the words of the *Book of Deuteronomy* which expressed the heart of his existence: "Hear, O Israel: the Lord our God is one Lord and you shall love the Lord your God with all your heart and with all your soul and with all your might" (6: 4-5). Jesus united into a single precept this commandment of love for God and the commandment of love for neighbor found in the *Book of Leviticus*: "You shall love your neighbor as yourself" (19: 18; cf. *Mk* 12: 29-31). Since God has first loved us (cf. *1 Jn* 4: 10), love is now no longer a mere "command"; it is the response to the gift of love with which God draws near to us.[lix]

As this is our last week of the Liturgical Year, it is most appropriate for us to reflect on the manner in which we have loved our Lord and the people our Lord has commissioned us to serve. We are called at the beginning of each liturgy to examine our consciences and reflect on the ways that we treat each other and treat our God, both good and bad. The end of each liturgical year and the beginning of the next year (starting with the First Sunday of Advent) often return to this theme of Judgment Day, focusing that judgment solely on the theme of God's love and the way that we utilize God's love within the world. Upon reflection, our lives often are more akin to that of a McRib and a Twinkie, this life of hedonistic pleasure and what's good for "me," rather than that of a good Christian steward. On many other occasions, I would like to think that our lives are based on removing our egos from what we do and allowing Christ to channel Himself through us, through the work of the Holy Spirit. Only when our motivation reflects God's motivation can we understand the power of this gospel message and the response to which we not only must respond but to which we choose to respond, always out of this love.

However we choose to love with the gifts that we have been given, let us freely and overflowing offer this love to others as God offers to us. Let us look beyond faith as a matter of sheep and goats and see our lives as a reflection and model of what God has done for us. For when we do that, we find great consolation in the words from the first letter of John which conclude this homily: "God is love and he who abides in love abides in God and God abides in him." This is our prayer.

Trinity Sunday (Ex 34: 4b-6, 8-9; Dn 3: 52, 53, 54, 55, 56; 2 Cor 13: 11-13; Jn 3: 16-18)

So as I have discussed with all of you already, my vacations away from the parish serve two purposes – they give me a chance to reenergize the batteries and they give the staff a chance to get rid of me for two weeks. Being the workaholic that I am, the only way the staff is assured that I won't come back to the parish is to throw me into the middle of a large body of water for two weeks without the use of cell phone or computer. On this particular trip that I recently took through Canada, I specifically committed myself to visit two specific places – Prince Edward Island and Montreal itself. I needed to visit Prince Edward Island because one of the bishop's former secretaries loves the "Anne of Green Gables" series and I went to the site where the books were inspired to take pictures for her, pick her up some Anne of Green Gables swag and to purchase homemade jellies for my staff at the parish. I visited Montreal because I did not go there last year and realized this might be my only chance to visit this beautifully clean French destination.

While in Montreal, the tour guide took us past the major sites – the old Montreal district, the Olympic Stadium and their version of a World Trade Center to name a few. We also made a couple stops on our tour, one of which serving as the inspiration for my homily – the Basilica of Notre Dame, located in the heart of the city.

Our tour guide informed us that the basilica of Notre Dame was constructed in the 1800s and was noted at the time as the largest church in North America. The church was designated as a basilica by St. Pope John Paul II in 1982 and we all know about the organ with the 7000 pipe range that adorns the balcony.

I was told that much of the architecture at the Montreal basilica was a mixture of various styles from the last few hundred years. I also was told that in the 1980s, a fire consumed a chapel that was built in the same style as the basilica and that the priests who pastored the basilica subsequently decided to rebuild the chapel in a more progressive style. The image of the Trinity was somewhat hidden within the bronze mural behind the altar but you had to spend a little time deciphering the mural before you could recognize the Trinitarian image.

Currently, the basilica is maintained by the Sulpician religious order. The Sulpician order happens to be close to my heart because I attended their seminary from 1985-1988 while studying philosophy in Washington, D.C. right across the street from the Basilica of the National Shrine of the Immaculate Conception.

After I listened intently about this basilica's specific history from our tour guide, my disposition somewhat changed from a tourist to the parish pastor. I made a promise to a few members of our community to pray for those who were sick and family members who have died. While the tour guide droned on about the history and magnificence of this basilica, I tuned myself out from what she was saying and spent a few quiet moments with the Lord (mind you, I eventually learned about the history of the basilica from the tour guide of the subsequent group that followed us – her English diction was a little easier to understand as well! ☺).

As soon as I tuned back to my current surroundings, I noticed that the tourists around me were busying themselves taking pictures of the beautiful imagery in the church. Mind you that I have often caught myself standing right next to these folks at times taking my share of pictures as well. However, for the sake of this homily, I realized how our lives are spent more taking the pictures of the images rather than allowing ourselves to enter the life of these images in the world of faith.

How often have we served as tourists in the world of faith rather than active participants? How often have we stood in the aisles of the pews gazing at the church's beauty rather than praying *in* the pews, investing ourselves in the life of prayer?

Look what has happened as a result of our collective Catholic population standing in outside of the churches or even in the aisles rather than investing themselves by fully, actively and consciously participating in Church life. In the United States, various media outlets have reported that those who were born after 1980 in this country (often referred to as "Millennials") have a tendency to push away institutional religion or the institution of marriage, focusing rather on individual fulfillment and the world of "the now." In my area, the decline of priestly vocations has reduced the priest/parishioner ratio to the levels of the early nineteenth century. After spending a week in Canada, I unfortunately have found out that the same lack of investment in the faith applies to this country as mine.

According to a report by the Canadian Broadcast Company of Nova Scotia (CBC), between the years of 1999-2014, the number of priests serving the diocese of Cape Breton has been cut almost in half (from 82 to 44). Immediate forecasts cite that the number of priests will drop to thirty within ten years covering more than 100 parishes. As a result, the diocese has decided to consolidate/close parishes to adjust to the priest change.

Some of those touring the city of Sydney were told last week that one of these parishes (Sacred Heart) would close by the end of the week I visited them.

This is the last of five parishes that have been closed for the purpose of consolidating all of them into one [the other four being St. Augustine's Church (which closed in July 2012), St. Nicholas' Church (July 2012), Immaculate Heart of Mira Road (June 2013) and St. Anthony Daniel (June 2014)].[lx]

Take the themes of Trinity Sunday, which is the focus of today's liturgy. How many times have we remembered viewing a sign at a given public event that reads "John 3: 16" without keeping to heart what "John 3: 16" actually means? It's a simple enough biblical verse that is easy enough to memorize and essential for our salvation: "For God so loved the world that He gave us His Only Son so those who believe might not perish but have eternal life."[lxi] To know the verse is good – to memorize the verse is better – to take the verse to heart and to live out the message will save our souls.

Take the image of the Trinity. If I took the scholarly route on this image, I could focus on the relationship between Father, Son and Holy Spirit via the teachings of two Church councils of the Fourth Century (Nicaea & I Constantinople) as well as the opposing views of this relationship as seen in the Eastern Orthodox and Roman Catholic Churches. If I took the non-scholarly approach to the subject, I could just tell you to take a look at the three connected circles that depict the Trinity and figure it out yourself. But I am a pastor and I have been taught by my community to use the homiletic approach of the KiSS ("Keep it Simple, Stupid). As I have done so many times in my own parish, let me try to explain the Trinity here, channeling a beautiful image from St. Augustine into this discussion[lxii].

You have two people in love. You have two people so in love that if they gaze into each other's eyes long enough, that they metaphorically enter into each other's souls and hearts. You realize that you are so deeply invested with the one that you love that you would rather be with them than with anyone else. When we experience that kind of love, a love that cannot be described simple in words but must be experienced, then we understand in a small way how the life of the Trinity exists. When we see couples in love, friends bonded together and most importantly married persons living out their sacrament, then we understand the love of the Trinity in some small way and our need to model that type of love with God to unite with God in this Christian cause.

Or we can just take a picture of an image of the Trinity in our minds like a tourist does this one day each year and just walk away...

Today we are called to make that investment in the faith with the same intensity and Christian love that God offers for us. May we learn of this love, invest in this love and then model this love of God by sharing it with the people that we meet. This is our prayer.

Corpus Christi (Dt 8: 2-3, 14b-16a; Ps 147: 12-13, 14-15, 19-20; 1 Cor 10: 16-17; Jn 6: 51-58)

My inspiration for today's homily took place at the local *Kentucky Fried Chicken* in Yorkville, Illinois. Over the years, I have grown to love fried chicken: Colonel Sander's, Popeye's and Joe's Greasy Spoon at the end of the block are a few of my favorite places. Partly, I like fried chicken for its flavor, but I think I live it more for its nostalgic value, knowing that my first experience of fried chicken took place at the high school seminary I attended in Madison, Wisconsin. The sisters who worked in the kitchen back in my high school seminary days were some of the holiest, most well-intentioned people I had ever met (and part of the reason why I became a priest). Because of their devotion to both the seminary and to the priestly life, I overcame the fact that they were pretty lousy cooks. Instead, I recalled this week the type of ministry that these women offered, a sacred one about which I very much wished to learn.

To be honest with you, the sisters tried very hard to serve quality food in the kitchen, but the results were not exactly in the realm of Wolfgang Puck. The delicacy of the house was their infamous fried bologna chunks. The deep fryer was the cooking device of choice. In my recollection of their cooking style, they would dip everything into a batter and throw it into hot oil. But everything they did began and ended with prayer and the sisters dedicated their lives to the well-being of every person they served.

Concerning their fried chicken, I was always interested in the way they prepared this particular meal, since the coating they used on the chicken resembled that of corn flakes but without any flavor whatsoever. Being that I couldn't figure out what kind of coating they were using, I asked the sisters one day what the secret was to making their version of fried chicken. The sisters replied to me that they received this secret coating, free of charge, from the Poor Clare Monastery from the southern end of the diocese.

To this day, the Poor Clares in Southern Wisconsin dedicate themselves to making altar breads for the surrounding parishes that place their orders with them. The bread is made from a simple batter of flour and water that is poured into a baking sheet and baked with simple designs. When the cooked sheet is cool enough to handle, the sisters punch out the hosts from the sheet and crumble the leftovers from the sheet. The sisters would take some of those crumbled remains from the baked product and ship to my high school seminary so that our sisters could use them as the coating for the fried chicken. No chicken could taste any blander than the chicken I tasted in Madison, Wisconsin.

In reality, the symbolism behind this simple flour and water recipe makes the feast of Corpus Christi that much more special in my own prayer life. Without adding anything to the flour and water, the bread sustains life, but not much else. I cannot help but think about our Old Testament brethren who wandered forty years in the wilderness during the great Exodus from the Old Testament. I thought about how these men and women ate this type of bland food for forty years, each and every day, a food which provided nourishment and strength for the journey, though in the eyes of the faithful, the food offered nothing more – the chosen people complained that the food was bland and their hope was low. The manna recalled the Exodus from Egypt, a flight that happened in such haste that those baking bread had no time to allow their own bread to rise. Like that great Exodus, the manna the chosen people ate did not have any flavor or texture. Without anything more within the bread, the bread itself became a simple function of living, but nothing more. (Mind you, the bread had a great symbolic effect of God's presence within a people who were led by the Lord out of slavery, but like a rich person who has everything but seeks more, the chosen men and women from the Old Testament wanted more, even though they had more than enough in their midst).

The bread we offer at the Presentation of the Gifts at Mass evokes the same themes as those of the Old Testament. A simple combination of flour and water, the bread that we offer seems lacking of taste and flavor. Without something added or changed to the recipe, the bread that we offer provides nothing more than nourishment to the body.

The beauty of this particular feast of Corpus Christi is that this particular bread will become different than any other bread we encounter in life. The key ingredient in this recipe is the presence of the Holy Spirit which changes the bread into something different, into the most sacred thing that exists in this world. When the Holy Spirit changes this bread, in appearance it looks like simple flour and water, but in reality, the form is changed into the Precious Body of our Lord, a presence that is neither bland nor simple.

Though a mystery never can be described adequately, what changes is the reality of that substance and the reality of the lives who receive it. Those who receive this gift no longer look at this changed Real Presence of Christ simply as a means by which the body is nourished but the soul as well. How many times in the scriptures has our Lord instructed the faithful concerning the spiritual gifts rendered through the reception of this gift? Jesus tells us in today's famous "Bread of Life" passage from the sixth chapter of John's Gospel, "I am the living bread that came down from heaven; whoever eats this bread will live forever; and the bread that I will give is my flesh for the life of the world."

Because of this change, the people who receive this bread are changed as well. The baptized who receive this presence of God alter their lives to model the presence they have received. Married couples become strengthened by this presence so that this presence may shine within their union and within their families. Those who live the gospel are strengthened to go out and preach the gospel, aided by that divine love in their hearts. Religious men and women who receive this gift become motivated to set the example of love, sometimes through the image of bad fried chicken to the people they encounter. It is through that example of love that the world sees the light of Christ shining brightly within the individual. It is through the presence of Christ that others are drawn to this table so that they may share this banquet with us.

As we gather at this table today, may we recognize the presence of God that changes this simple bread and wine into something necessary for our lives and our salvation. May we understand the reality of the Real Presence, may we embrace it and invite others to come around this table to share it with us. This is our prayer.

Endnotes

[i] R. E. Brown, J. A. Fitzmyer & R. E. Murphy, <u>The Jerome Biblical Commentary, Vol. 2</u>, (Englewood Cliffs, NJ: Prentice-Hall, 1996), p. 106

[ii] <u>A Select Library of the Nicene and Post-Nicene Fathers of the Christian Church, Volume VIII</u>, ed. Philip Schaff (Grand Rapids, MI: Wm B. Eerdmans Publishing Company, 1996), p. 128.

[iii] 2 Sm 10-12.

[iv] Jer 24: 5-7

[v] <u>From a sermon by Pope St. Leo the Great, pope</u> (Sermo 1 in Nativitate Domini, 1-3: PI, 54). The Catholic Church, <u>The Divine Office: The Liturgy of the Hours According to the Roman Rite (Volume I) as Renewed by Decree of the Second Vatican Council and Promulgated by the Authority of Pope Paul</u> (New York: Catholic Book Publishing Company, 1975), pp. 190-193

[vi] Psalm 51: 9-15.

[vii] St. Thérèse of Lisieux, "The Little Flower," <u>The Poems of St. Thérèse of Lisieux</u> (n.d.) in *Catholic First* retrieved September 2, 2014 from http://catholicfirst.com/thefaith/catholicclassics/stther ese/poemsofsttherese06a.html

[viii] St. Pope John Paul II, "Homily to the Faithful of Mbabane, Swaziland," retrieved September 16, 1988 from http://w2.vatican.va/content/john-paul-ii/en/homilies/1988/documents/hf_jp-ii_hom_19880916_mbabane.html

[ix] M. F. Toal, <u>The Sunday Sermons of the Great Fathers (Vol. 1)</u> (Swedesboro, NJ: Preservation Press, 1996) p. 203.

[x] Rev. Walter Ciszek, S.J., "Doing God's Will," excerpt

from He Leadeth Me (San Francisco, CA: Ignatius Press, 1973), pp. 158-159.

[xi] Post-Synodal Apostolic Exhortation **Vita Consecrata** of the Holy Father St. John Paul II to the bishops and clergy, religious orders and congregation's societies of apostolic life, secular institutes and all the faithful on the consecrated life and its mission in the Church and in the world (Vatican City: Libreria Editrice Vaticana, 1996), #14, 15.

[xii] Attributed to St. Patrick of Ireland (n.d.) in *Brainy Quotes* retrieved March 29, 2014 from http://www.brainyquote.com/quotes/quotes/s/saintpatri189990.html.

[xiii] Jn 14: 1-6.

[xiv] St. Melito of Sardis (n.d.), "Homily on the Passover" in *Cogwriter*, retrieved April 18, 2014 from http://www.cogwriter.com/melitohomily.htm.

[xv] Ibid.

[xvi] "Good Friday Evening Prayer," The Divine Office: Liturgy of the Hours, Volume II, p. 491.

[xvii] Aesop (n.d.), "The Father, His Son and a Bundle of Sticks," in *Fables of Aesop,* retrieved April 19, 2014 from http://fablesofaesop.com/the-father-his-sons-and-the-bundle-of-sticks.html

[xviii] Pope Francis (January 15, 2014), "General Audience" in Vatican Website, retrieved April 19, 2014 from http://w2.vatican.va/content/francesco/es/audiences/2014/documents/papa-francesco_20140115_udienza-generale.html

[xix] Dr. Seuss, Green Eggs and Ham (New York, NY: Random House, 1960).

[xx] R. F. Moran (1911), St. Patrick. In The Catholic Encyclopedia (New York: Robert Appleton Company, 2014), retrieved September 2, 2014 from New Advent: http://www.newadvent.org/cathen/11554a.htm

xxi Psalm 23.
xxii International Commission on English in the Liturgy, The Rites of the Catholic Church, Volume II (Collegeville, MN: The Liturgical Press, 1991), pp. 34-35.
xxiii The Jerome Biblical Commentary, p. 453.
xxiv Dn 7: 9
xxv St. Athanasius, On the Incarnation (Crestwood, NY: St. Vladimir's Seminary Press, 1998), p. 65.
xxvi See http://www.foxbusiness.com/industries/2013/12/31/retailers-brace-for-change-ahead-incandescent-bulb-ban/
xxvii Mt 5: 11-12
xxviii 1 Cor 1: 28-29
xxix Second Vatican Council, Dogmatic Constitution on the Church, *Lumen Gentium* (Vatican II, November 21, 1964; Northport, NY: Costello Publishing Co., 1996), n. 33.
xxx Lk 12: 11-12.
xxxi Phil 4: 4-7
xxxii Edward P. Sri, "The Feathers of Gossip: How our Words can Build Up or Tear Down," *Lay Witness Magazine* (Sept/Oct, 2010).
xxxiii 2 Cor 11: 30.
xxxiv Ps 23: 4.
xxxv Mt 5: 11.
xxxvi St. Thérèse of Lisieux, "Nada te turbe" (Copyright © 1986, 1991 by Ateliers et Presses de Taizé, F-71250 Taizé Community, France). Published in North America by GIA Publications, Inc., 7404 S. Mason Ave., Chicago, IL 60638
xxxvii St. Theresa of Avila, The Way to Perfection, retrieved September 2, 2014 from Clerus.org: http://www.clerus.org/bibliaclerusonline/en/dmh.htm

xxxviii Zc 9: 9.

xxxix Mt 11: 25, 28.

xl Pope Francis, "Meeting with the Clergy: Palatine Chapel in the Royal Palace of Caserta - Saturday, 26 July 2014," retrieved August 3, 2014 from the Vatican Website: http://w2.vatican.va/content/francesco/en/speeches/2014/july/documents/papa-francesco_20140726_clero-caserta.html

xli On the www.vatican.va, the transcript is only provided in Italian and German. I passed this dialogue through a translation program online; the accuracy of this quotation might be suspect. For the original transcript in Italian, please go to http://w2.vatican.va/content/francesco/it/speeches/2014/august/documents/papa-francesco_20140805_ministranti-tedeschi.html for more information).

xlii Pope Francis, "Meeting with Altar Boys from Germany," (translated by Peter Jankowski... badly) retrieved August 6, 2014 from Vatican Website: http://w2.vatican.va/content/francesco/it/speeches/2014/august/documents/papa-francesco_20140805_ministranti-tedeschi.html

xliii "Official Prayer Attributed to St. Maria Goretti," retrieved September 2, 2014 from Catholic Culture Website: http://www.catholicculture.org/culture/liturgicalyear/prayers/view.cfm?id=1075

xliv Scott McGuire, "How were the adult's "mwa-mwa-mwa" voices made?" retrieved on September 2, 2014 at The Peanuts' Animation and Video Page: http://fivecentsplease.org/tv/peanuts-tv.html

xlv Mt 5: 37.

xlvi Mark Jennings, "Mt. Everest – The Mess at the Top of the World," Reader's Digest, October 2013, retrieved

September 2, 2014 at the Reader's Digest Website: http://www.rd.com/true-stories/survival/everest-the-mess-at-the-top-of-the-world/

xlvii Pope St. John XXIII, "First Discourse at the Second Vatican Council" (1962), retrieved at the Vatican Website: http://www.vatican.va/holy_father/john_xxiii/speeches/1962/documents/hf_j-xxiii_spe_19621011_opening-council_it.html.Translated on the Vatican Website from Pope Blessed Paul VI's "Final Discourse at the Second Vatican Council" (1965) at http://www.vatican.va/holy_father/paul_vi/speeches/1965/documents/hf_p-vi_spe_19651207_epilogo-concilio_en.html

xlviii George Washington, "Letter to Colonel Bassett, Mount Vernon," April 25, 1773; *The Writings of George Washington*, collected and edited by Worthington Chauncey Ford (New York and London: G. P. Putnam's Sons, 1889). Vol. II (1758-1775)

xlix Abraham Lincoln, "National Thanksgiving: A Proclamation by the President of the United States of America," Published in The New York Times – October 5, 1863, retrieved from the New York Times Website: http://www.nytimes.com/1863/10/05/news/national-thanksgiving-proclamation-president-united-states-america.html

l Pope Benedict XVI, General Audience – September 17, 2008, retrieved September 9, 2014 at the Vatican Website: http://www.vatican.va/holy_father/benedict_xvi/audiences/2008/documents/hf_ben-xvi_aud_20080917_en.html

li Mt 22: 21.

lii Pope St. John XXIII, "Speech to the Moon" on the First Evening of the Second Vatican Council - October 11,

1962, retrieved from the Whispers of the Loggia Website: http://whispersintheloggia.blogspot.com/2011_10_01_archive.html

[liii] Second Vatican Council, Pastoral Constitution on the Church in the Modern World, *Gaudium et Spes* (Vatican II, December 7, 1965; Northport, NY: Costello Publishing Co., 1996), n. 27.

[liv] Ibid, n. 27.

[lv] Mt 28: 18-20.

[lvi] Hans Urs von Balthasar, "A Résumé of my Thought (Translated by Kelly Hamilton, Communio Magazine 15 (Winter 1988), retrieved September 2, 2014 at the Ignatius Insight Website: http://www.ignatiusinsight.com/features2005/print2005/hub_resume_print.html

[lvii] Ibid.

[lviii] Chris Gayomali, "What is the McRib Made of Anyway?" November 14, 2013, retrieved from The Week Website: http://theweek.com/article/index/220866/whats-the-mcrib-made-of-anyway

[lix] Pope Benedict XVI, Encyclical "Deus Caritas Est," December 25, 2005, retrieved September 2, 2014 at the Vatican Website: http://www.vatican.va/holy_father/benedict_xvi/encyclicals/documents/hf_ben-xvi_enc_20051225_deus-caritas-est_en.html

[lx] Canadian Broadcast Company, "Diocese Confirms several Cape Breton churches to Close" in Canada MSN News, retrieved June 20, 2014 from http://news.ca.msn.com/local/novascotia/diocese-confirms-several-cape-breton-churches-to-close

[lxi] St. Augustine's Love Sermon #110. Website: https://www.christianhistoryinstitute.org/study/module/augustine/

Bibliography

Scripture texts in this work are taken from the *New American Bible, revised edition* © 2010, 1991, 1986, 1970 Confraternity of Christian Doctrine, Washington, D.C. and are used by permission of the copyright owner. All Rights Reserved. No part of the New American Bible may be reproduced in any form without permission in writing from the copyright owner.
Catholic Church. *Catechism of the Catholic Church*. Vatican City: Libreria Editrice Vaticana.

(Attributed), St. Patrick. *On Humiliation*. From Website Attributed to St. Patrick of Ireland (n.d). retrieved March 29, 2014 from the Brainy Quote Website: http://www.brainyquote.com/quotes/quotes/s/saintpatri189990.html.

Aesop. *The Father, His Sons and a Bundle of Sticks*. Retrieved September 12, 2014 at the Aesop Fable Website: http://fablesofaesop.com/the-father-his-sons-and-the-bundle-of-sticks.html, n.d.

Athanasius, St. *On the Incarnation*. Crestwood, NY: St. Vladimir's Seminary Press, 1998.

Avila, St. Teresa of. *Way to Perfection*. Retrieved at the Biblia Clerus Website: http://www.clerus.org/bibliaclerusonline/en/dmh.ht, n.d.

Balthasar, Hans Urs von. *"A Résumé of my Thought (Translated by Kelly Hamilton, Communio Magazine 15*. Retrieved September 2, 2014 at the Ignatius Insight Website: http://www.ignatiusinsight.com/features2005/print2005/hub_resume_print.html

Pope Benedict XVI. *Encyclical "Deus Caritas Est"*. Retrieved at the Vatican Website:

http://www.vatican.va/holy_father/benedict_xvi/encyclicals/documents/hf_ben-xvi_enc_20051225_deus-caritas-est_en.html, 2005.

—. *General Audience - September 17, 2008.* Vatican City: Retrieved at the Vatican Website: http://www.vatican.va/holy_father/benedict_xvi/audiences/2008/documents/hf_ben-xvi_aud_20080917_en.html, 2008.

Brown, Raymond and R. E. Murphy. *The Jerome Biblical commentary (Vol. 2).* Englewood Cliffs, NJ: : Prentice-Hall, 1996.

The Catholic Church. *The Divine Office: The Liturgy of the Hours According to the Roman Rite : as Renewed by Decree of the Second Vatican Council and Promulgated by the Authority of Pope Paul.* New York: Catholic Book Publishing Company, 1975.

Ciszek, Rev. Walter. "Doing God's Will," excerpt from *He Leadeth Me.* San Francisco, CA: Ignatius Press, 1973.

The Canadian Broadcast Company. *Diocese Confirms Several Cape Breton Churches to Close.* Retrieved June 30, 2014 from the Canadian Broadcast Website: http://news.ca.msn.com/local/novascotia/diocese-confirms-several-cape-breton-churches-to-close, 2013.

The International Commission on English in the Liturgy. *The Rites of the Catholic Church, Volume II.* Collegeville, MN: The Liturgical Press, 1991.

Jennings, Mark. *"Mt. Everest – The Mess at the Top of the World," Reader's Digest.* Retrieved September 2, 2014 at the Reader's Digest Website: http://www.rd.com/true-stories/survival/everest-the-mess-at-the-top-of-the-world/, 2013.

Mershman, F. The Catholic Encyclopedia. New York: Robert Appleton Company, 1912.

Pope St. John XXIII. *"Speech to the Moon," Address on the First Evening of the Second Vatican Council*

(October 11, 1962). Vatican City: Retrieved at the Whispers of the Loggia Website: http://whispersintheloggia.blogspot.com/2011_10_01_archive.html, 1962.

—. *First Discourse of the Second Vatican Council.* Vatican City: Retrieved at Vatican Website http://www.vatican.va/holy_father/john_xxiii/speeches/1962/documents/hf_j-xxiii_spe_19621011_opening-council_it.html., 1962. Translated on Vatcian Website in Pope Blessed Paul VI's Final Discourse on the Second Vatican Council at http://www.vatican.va/holy_father/paul_vi/speeches/1965/documents/hf_p-vi_spe_19651207_epilogo-concilio_en.html.

(Attributed to) St. Maria Goretti. *"Official Prayer Attributed to St. Maria Goretti"*. Retrieved September 2014 from the Catholic Culture Website: http://www.catholicculture.org/culture/liturgicalyear/prayers/view.cfm?id=1075.

McGuire, Scott. *"How were the adult's "mwa-mwa-mwa" voices made?"*. Retrieved September 2, 2014 from The Peanuts' Animation and Video Page: http://fivecentsplease.org/tv/peanuts-tv.html.

St. Melito of Sardis. *Homily on the Passover*. Retrieved September 12, 2014 from the Cogwriter Website: http://www.cogwriter.com/melitohomily.htm., n.d.

"About St. Patrick," *The Catholic Encyclopedia*. Moran, P.F. (1911). St. Patrick. In The Catholic Encyclopedia. Retrieved September 2, 2014 from New Advent Website: http://www.newadvent.org/cathen/11554a.htm, 2014.

Pope Francis. *"Meeting with the Clergy: Palatine Chapel in the Royal Palace of Caserta - Saturday, 26 July 2014,"* . Caserta, Italy: Retrieved August 3, 2014 from the Vatican Website:

http://w2.vatican.va/content/francesco/en/speeches/2014/july/documents/papa-francesco_2014, 2014.

—. "Meeting with Altar Boys from Germany," (translated by Peter Jankowski... badly). Vatican City: Retrieved August 6, 2014 from Vatican Website: http://w2.vatican.va/content/francesco/it/speeches/2014/august/documents/papa-francesco_20140805_ministranti-tedesc, 2014.

—. "General Audience" from January 15, 2014. Retrieved April 19, 2014 from the Vatican Website: //w2.vatican.va/content/francesco/es/audiences/2014/documents/papa-francesco_20140115_udienza-generale.html

Pope St. John Paul II. *Post-Synodal Apostolic Exhortation*. Vatican City: Libreria Editrice Vaticana, 1996.

Second Vatican Council. *Vatican Council II: Constitutions, Decrees, Declarations: Dogmatic Constitution of the Church, Lumen Gentium*. Northport, NY: Costello Publishing Company, 1964, 1996.

Seuss, Dr. *Green Eggs and Ham*. New York, NY: Random House, 1960.

Sri, Edward. *"The Feathers of Gossip: How our Words Can Build Up or Tear Down," Lay Witness Magazine*. September/October 2010.

St. Theresa of Avila, The Way to Perfection. Retrieved September 2, 2014 from the Clerus.org Website: http://www.clerus.org/bibliaclerusonline/en/dmh.htm

St. Thèrése of Lisieux. *"The Little Flower," The Poems of St. Thérèse of Lisieux*. Retrieved September 2, 2014 from The Catholic First Website: http://catholicfirst.com/thefaith/catholicclassics/sttherese/poemsofstthereseo6a.html, (n.d.).

-----. *"Nada te turbe"*. France: Taizé Community

(Published in North America by GIA Publications, Inc., 7404 S. Mason Ave., Chicago, IL 60638), 1986, 1991.

Toal, M. F. *The Sunday Sermons of the Great Fathers (Vols. 1-4)*. Swedesboro, NJ: Preservation Press, 1996.

Washington, George. *"Letter to Colonel Bassett, Mount Vernon, April 25, 1773,"* The Writings of George Washington, collected and edited by Worthington Chauncey Ford, Vol. II (1758-1775). New York & London: G. P. Putnam's Sons, 1889, 1889.

About the Author

As a priest of the Joliet Diocese since 1996, Fr. Pete Jankowski received his Bachelor's Degree in Philosophy at the Catholic University of America (Washington, DC) and his Master's Degree in Divinity and Licentiate in Sacred Theology at the University of St. Mary of the Lake (Mundelein, IL). Fr. Pete has celebrated the sacraments in all seven counties of the Joliet Diocese, both for the English and Spanish speaking communities. Since 2006, Fr. Pete has served as pastor of St. Patrick's Church (Joliet, IL), chaplain at Stateville Maximum Security Prison in Crest Hill, IL and as an Adjunct Professor of Theology at the University of St. Francis in Joliet.

St. Patrick's Church is noted as the oldest Catholic Church in Northern Illinois (since 1838). With his trusty pain in the neck dog Rusty at his side (he's a sixty-pound Basset Hound and he's all trouble), Fr. Pete spends his days taking care of the wonderful folks of the parish and community. In his spare time (_what_ spare time?) Fr. Pete enjoys writing poetry and music. He also spends a good deal of time with his family.

www.ingramcontent.com/pod-product-compliance
Lightning Source LLC
Chambersburg PA
CBHW052015070526
44584CB00016B/1759